Book Four in the
On a Wing and a Prayer series

Such Sweet Songs

The song of a bird can heal a wounded heart

Linda Franklin

TEACH Services, Inc.
PUBLISHING
www.TEACHServices.com • (800) 367-1844

World rights reserved. This book or any portion thereof may not be copied or reproduced in any form or manner whatever, except as provided by law, without the written permission of the publisher, except by a reviewer who may quote brief passages in a review.

The author assumes full responsibility for the accuracy of all facts and quotations as cited in this book. The opinions expressed in this book are the author's personal views and interpretations, and do not necessarily reflect those of the publisher.

This book is provided with the understanding that the publisher is not engaged in giving spiritual, legal, medical, or other professional advice. If authoritative advice is needed, the reader should seek the counsel of a competent professional.

Copyright © 2018 Linda Franklin
Copyright © 2018 TEACH Services, Inc.
ISBN-13: 978-1-4796-0945-1 (Paperback)
ISBN-13: 978-1-4796-0946-8 (ePub)
Library of Congress Control Number: 2018938993

Never before published true and inspirational bird stories!

Edited by Linda May Harrington Steinke

Scriptures are taken from the King James Version of the Bible. Public domain.

Photos by Linda Franklin and online stock.

Published by

www.TEACHServices.com • (800) 367-1844

Other books by Linda Franklin

On a Wing and a Prayer series

Book One: *Just a Little Higher*—Comfort comes on soft little wings just when these women need it most!

Book Two: *Staying Aloft*—True stories about men and the extraordinary birds who loved them.

Book Three: *Climbing the Heights*—Never before published true and inspirational bird stories.

Rainbow series

Book One: *Rainbow in the Flames*—A tragic fire, a bow of promise, a love of the lasting kind. The healing journey of an optimistic burn survivor (color photos).

Book Two: *Shadows Point to Rainbows*—A dog and his boy strengthen each other.

Book Three: *Johnny Sundown*—A wild trapper discovers solace in Canada's Peace Country.

Survival series

Book One: *Country in My Heart*—Success stories of people who prayed for a country home. Compiled and edited by Jere and Linda Franklin (b/w photos).

Dedication

This book is gratefully dedicated to

Bea Kurjata

Whenever I take time for a visit with Bea, she speaks as if reading to me from a pre-edited script, so precise, deliberate, and appropriate are her comments. She often includes poems memorized in childhood (Resurrection, page 39). No writer could have a more enthusiastic supporter, faithful distributor, nor magneloquent (her word) storyteller as a friend. Thanks, Bea!

Contents

A Naturalist's Observation . . . . *vii*

Introduction . . . . *ix*

Stories

One Stick at a Time 13

Sir Winston 23

Bluebird in My Path 39

Mourning Lullaby 43

Yellow Bird 55

Song of Peace 63

I Heard, I Listened 67

Skip to Me, Lou! 73

Troubadour 81

Prisoners of Hope 93

The Weaver 101

Angels Camp Fire 107

White Crown 115

Poems and Quotations

Melody of Praise—*Ellen G. White* 20

Cleaning Concepts 22

Hearing His Voice—*Ellen G. White* .37

Service—*Edgar A. Guest* 38

Joyful Trust—*Ellen G. White* 42

Resurrection—*Anon* 53

Creation—*Edgar A. Guest* 54

Sympathy—*Paul Laurence Dunbar* 62

The Ark and the Dove— *H. P. Nichols* 66

Singing in the Dark—*Ellen G. White* 70

The Frail Bird's Song—*Mary K. Donesky* 71

Unnumbered Immensity—*Ellen G. White* 72

To a Skylark—*Percy B. Shelley* 77

Genius—*Edgar A. Guest* 92

Hope—*Emily Dickenson* 99

Possession—*Edgar A. Guest* 100

What the Robin Told—*Anon* 113

The Little Bird—*Anon* 114

God, the Artist— *Angela Morgan* 120

Bird Words 122

Sweet Lesson of Trust—*Ellen G. White* 123

A Naturalist's Observation

Blessed are your eyes, for they see: and your ears, for they hear.

—Matthew 13:16

"Cheer [a friendly wild red-winged blackbird] had us up the next morning at dawn. It was well he did, for there was much to be done that day. As if he had known that, he flew to our bedroom window, perched on a convenient tree and called to us in a manner that left no doubt of his motive. He wanted us to get up... .

"What more pleasant manner of awakening could there be than to the musical notes of this blessed feathered alarm clock!

"How do such animals know [when we are planning to leave]? How keen is their intuition and their understanding of circumstances? I am always stymied by these questions. There is the fear in answering them that we give creatures credit for either too much or too little intelligence. But certain it is that there is a character very deep and profound in these living things with which we share the world, and we glimpse a bit of their true nature only when our attitude is kindly, patient and anxious to understand."

— From *The Living Forest Series*, by Sam Campbell

Introduction

In January of 2007, *The Washington Post* hired a violinist to play for an hour at a Metro station in Washington, DC. An estimated crowd of two-thousand people rushed through the station, not so much as slowing their pace. Several toddlers and young children tried to stop and listen, but their parents urged them forward. The musician's hat accumulated $32. The violinist, Joshua Bell, one of the world's greatest musicians, had played the same music (some of the most intricate pieces ever written by Bach), with the same violin (worth $3.5 million dollars), to a crowd in a Boston theatre just the week before. Each seat averaged $100.

Surround Sound

Like the folks at the Metro station, we can become deaf to the beautiful, joyful music surrounding us in the form of bird's songs. There are as many reasons for this lack of appreciation as there are people—loss of wonder, tight schedules, preoccupation, and activities that prevent quietness. I appreciate the songs of birds, having held many wounded birds and watched them rejoin their fellows with (what I believe to be) a chirp of appreciation. Now, I can't even ignore the sparrows who sing in the rafters at Costco!

A bird's song is an intricate accomplishment, physiologically, but its value is not solely in execution. Like love, friendship, and all of the other truly valuable possessions, a song cannot be defined in monetary terms. Music is a connection possessed by those who are capable of receiving it. Step out of the Metro—lean in and listen—for your soul's sake.

When Birds Sing

Early in the day the songs of the birds tend to be lively, louder, and repeated more frequently. Males and females both sing, but the males have more volume and vocalize more often. With the exception of nocturnal birds of prey, most birds will not sing at night. A diurnal bird will rarely make an exception to their rule of nighttime quietude (as in *Angels Camp* in this volume, and *Rainbow in the Dark*, in Book One of this series). Neither do they sing during their summer molt because they do not want to reveal their presence. During their time of new feathering, they are weak and vulnerable to predators.

Why Birds Sing

Birds sing for many reasons: defending territory, attracting a mate, courtship duets, communication—in thankfulness for the sheer joy of living. Fledglings learn the types of language of their species from their parents: conversational, disciplinary, contented mutterings, raucous scolding of enemies, clear and melodious songs that mature with age.

How Birds Sing

The voice-box of a bird is different from mammals in that it has an added section at the lower end of the trachea, or windpipe. Where the bronchi join the trachea is an organ called a syrinx, with specialized muscles that control the tension on the membranes. By varying the frequency (pitch) and intensity (volume) of air passing from the lungs through the tracheal structure, the song is formed. Birds without a syrinx cannot sing (vultures and some storks). The more syringeal muscles that are present, the wider the variety of possible songs produced. The syrinx also enables a bird to sing more than one tone at a time.

For many years it was supposed that baby birds learned their song by parental example, but the complexities of song formation have only recently been scientifically proven in an experiment with zebra finches (*Taeniopygia guttata*) in *BMC Genomics*. Genes that were once considered non-essential are now tagged with significance as part of a complex voice regulatory network. When the young male finch hears his father's song, his genetic network is triggered, and neurochemicals are released in his immature brain. The regulation of microRNAs in high-order auditory parts of the zebra finch brain appear to be unique to birds. So it has been concluded that the zebra finch carries possible key regulators of song-triggered gene networks.

Inter-species Communication

There are amusing reports of mimicry among birds who speak or sing in human language and repeat mechanical sounds. Some birds can verbalize meaningful phrases at appropriate times; one lost budgie repeated his home address to the Japanese police and was returned to his overjoyed owner who had taken time to instruct her bird. Others have been taught to identify specific objects when asked. Yet, within the past fifteen years it has become obvious to me that there is a more significant category of avian communication; birds deliver messages that humans comprehend in times of crisis.

The inner ear is quickened by the precision tool of EOHS—emotional open-heart surgery. One person is deaf to tones that enliven someone else. Just as a microscope reveals a whole new world to the human eye, so a birdsong may only be appreciated with the assistance of EOHS.

Such Sweet Songs

King David's richest songs were written when his heart was laid bare, when he was repentant, in great need of God's assistance. The "sweet singer of Israel" knew the healing virtue of song.

This fourth volume of the *On a Wing and a Prayer* series, like the other three books, is carefully hemmed by that beloved admonition that saves us from blind imaginings; whatsoever things are true, honest, just, pure, lovely, of good report, virtuous, and absolutely full of praise!

Before you begin reading, I challenge you to consider my new hypothesis: "For those who can hear it, there is healing in the song of a bird."

> *In singing bird and opening blossom,*
> *in rain and sunshine,*
> *in summer breeze and gentle dew,*
> *in ten thousand objects in nature,*
> *from the oak of the forest*
> *to the violet that blossoms at its root,*
> *is seen the love that restores.*

—Education, p. 101

One Stick at a Time

*For the thing which I greatly feared is come upon me,
and that which I was afraid of is come unto me.*

—Job 3:25

The busy catbird never knew that the cheerful songs it "sang into the air" that spring day lodged in a needy heart. It was Isabelle's* first, and perhaps most difficult, year as a pastor's wife. Plagued with weakness from physical illness, she was overwhelmed, this particular day, with duties she felt incapable of surmounting. She'd had a late start that morning, loathe to face the mountain of tasks, when unfamiliar, heavenly music floated through her window, blessing and uplifting her. Long years afterward, at the times she is most in need of it, the message of that song still speaks to her, still whispers its gentle encouragement.

The bright, warm morning rays of the spring sunshine streaming through the bedroom window failed to calm my anxious spirit as I rehearsed again the numerous duties that flitted helter-skelter through my mind. Where should I begin? Which was most important? How could I complete all the tasks expected? How do I sort them all out? Maybe I can't! Maybe I'm just a failure.

The fears that had begun creeping into my thinking as my husband and I drove our two old cars across the nation a few months before, to his new pastoral assignment, were now becoming a stark reality. When the call had first come to Douglas* to pastor in Kentucky, we had practically danced around the room for joy. I knew that it fulfilled some intense longings in his heart, and I was eager to join him in them. He was longing to get back into pastoring, and to live in Kentucky! Could it be we were actually to embark on this new life together? It hardly seemed possible.

New Beginnings

After working for several years as a single Bible worker (and sometimes as a pastor), my husband had surprised his friends by finally shedding his image as a confirmed bachelor as we joyfully united our lives in matrimony. We were eager to start this new ministry as a pastoral couple, but there were a few, very big question marks that plagued me. We still felt like newly-weds, but we had already faced some major challenges in our few years together. Only a few months before receiving this call to Kentucky, I'd had surgery for cancer, and I was still struggling with the fear that in just a few months I would be on my deathbed. I feared I would be imposing grief and pain on our new congregation if they had to watch the new pastor's wife die. Yet, at the same time I wondered, *Could it be that this call was God's intimation that instead of dying, I would live? Was He inviting me to begin a new adventure?* That possibility filled me with hope and eager expectation.

The Perfect Wife

As Doug and I neared our new district, however, other nameless fears began to take on a definite shape. It seemed to me that a pastor's wife belonged to a different class of human beings than the one I belonged to. I "knew" that a pastor's wife was expected to be "perfect," a wonderful cook, an organizer, always ready for any amount of company, a gracious hostess, capable of leading out in any church assignment with poise and dignity, impeccably and appropriately dressed for every occasion, and, of course, had immaculate housekeeping skills. As the miles ticked by, I struggled with my fears and prayed—often aloud. One comforting answer tried to calm my heart. "Isabelle, forget about your fears, just love the people." But the closer we got to the district, the bigger my fears grew. It seemed to me that I possessed none of the skills I needed in order to be a pastor's wife.

This perfect wife, I would soon learn, seemed to exactly fit the description of the pretty, young pastor's wife who had just left the district to which we were assigned! Not only did she possess all those skills that came so hard for me, she was a talented interior decorator, and a hairdresser to boot! Every Sabbath I heard yet another story about the woman they were missing. She sounded so vivacious, energetic, confident, and well-loved that I felt more and more like a misguided transplant—like a cactus in a lily pond.

Our house was an unfurnished skeleton, and it would take some time before we would have the money needed to change that. We didn't even have a bed or a dresser yet—only a borrowed mattress on the floor and some cardboard drawers I bought at a dollar store. Our off-colored hand-me-down love seat was swallowed by the huge living room. From a thrift store we had picked up some well-worn easy chairs and an old card table for eating our meals. Besides this we had an enormous clunker of a piano, an ungainly desk, and some huge, ugly particle-board shelving for books. And boxes! Eleven thousand of them! (well, not quite)—mostly books. Whatever I needed was always in the bottom box!

Even if we'd had money, though, I knew nothing about room decor. Niceties had been strangers in my childhood home. As for clothing, I had comfortable dresses, but they didn't seem to be the quality that a "pastor's wife" ought to wear. I coveted skills that would enable me to make tasty dishes and serve them on an elegant tablecloth with fine china, silver, and candles, but I didn't even know how to drape a window properly, and I was afraid to share my cooking with anyone.

When we moved to our new district, I feared what would happen when our congregation discovered my ineptitude. I didn't have to wait long. Our house was on a main road and hardly a day passed without church members dropping in unexpectedly. They had to walk through my messy kitchen to get to the living room. Even though there were only two of us, I somehow managed to always have a mess in the kitchen! I remember one lady looking around at my chaos (I was preparing for Vacation Bible School at the time) and saying with wide-open arms and great delight, "Wonderful! Wonderful! You can come to my house any time!" At least no one in our congregation would ever be tempted to feel intimidated about their own housekeeping skills because of me!

Besides the house, however, I had other duties. My pastor husband liked to have me go with him to hospital visits, Bible studies, and other pastoral visits. Sometimes I was needed to care for overnight guests, help with funeral planning, or take some of the lengthy phone calls (most of them from parishioners who just needed someone to listen to them, but were often complicated by personal and interpersonal problems). He also liked to have my help with some of his projects, especially book writing. Then he decided to produce a radio program at home—but he needed someone to set up the equipment, do the recording, edit the tapes, and copy them. I tried in vain to make those programs sound professional with non-professional equipment—and then there were a few Bible correspondence students generated by that program to care for. At first, I attended every church meeting, and I was often needed to play the piano or even to sing in an emergency. Both of these tasks were nerve-wracking to me. It seemed as if I played the piano and sang about the same way I kept house—not with proficiency and joy—but with an uneasy sense of fear that I just wasn't good enough.

The Perfect Mess

In my eagerness to be a "good pastor's wife" I hardly thought about caring for myself, or that I was still in recovery from a life-threatening illness that had left me thin and weak. I did not know that other health problems were already taking their toll on my strength as well. I didn't understand that not only was it OK, but that it was very important for me to have more restful, joyful, relaxing times if I wanted to recover and thrive and have the ability to refresh others.

I wasn't complaining; I wanted to do those things—all of them, and more, but I had no clue how to organize and manage my time and take on realistic loads. I enjoyed the ministry-related activities. They seemed so important that it was easy to let the housekeeping chores slide. The uneasy anxiety about my failures as a homemaker made *my* work stressful, while *his* projects seemed so much more interesting. But as things built up, I became anxious to stay home and try to organize things. When I did, however, the job seemed bigger than life. I didn't know where to begin.

Today was one of those uneasy, stay-at-home days, where all the evidences of my failures mocked my efforts to bring order. I caught a glimpse of my face in the mirror, and I saw through the looking glass darkly. The chaos and worry in my mind had painted a black cloud on my face. But that day, in the mix of confusing, dark thoughts, sweet music drifted through the window to me and pierced my darkness like brilliant rays of sunshine in a cave.

It was the clear, happy notes of a songbird. Even though I felt frustrated and harried, the bird-lover in me couldn't resist the urge to figure out what kind of bird was singing. I puzzled over the melody. Who was the musician? It wasn't a robin or a wood thrush. It sounded a little bit like a mockingbird, but not quite. Perhaps it was a brown thrasher? Curiosity pulled me to the bedroom window.

A small tree stood by my window (I later discovered it to be a Rose of Sharon bush). Through its branches I could still see the lofty trees and spring flowers in the back yard, bordered by a peacefully flowing river. The refreshing scene never failed to draw my mind away from my troubles and remind me of our loving Creator. A quick movement very close to my window, in the Rose of Sharon bush, caught my eye. There was the sweet singer pouring a melody from her little heart! She wasn't strikingly beautiful, just a charcoal gray, robin-sized bird with a black cap and a bit of rust color under her tail. A catbird! I had not seen a catbird in Kentucky until that day.

The Perfect Answer

I listened to her song for a few moments until she flitted away with the characteristic meowing call that gave her her name. I had enjoyed finding the bird, but without giving it much thought I went back to work on my morning chores.

Mrs. Catbird wasn't through with me yet, however. She had a lesson for me that would take time to unfold. Several times throughout that day, I heard her song. Peeking out the window, I would find her sitting briefly in the same tree, singing. To my delight, it finally dawned on me that she was building her nest right there in the Rose of Sharon bush—right where I could watch her through my bedroom window as she raised her young. I was thrilled!

Back and forth she came throughout the day, building her home, one stick at a time. Each time she placed a stick, she called me to the window with one more stanza of her house-building song. Had she come just to encourage me? As I watched, this little "fowl of the air" began to teach me. As each small task was completed, she stopped to sing out the joy that inspired her to sing.

When the significance of her actions began to reach my heart, I stood rooted to the spot, captivated by the new concept that began to dawn on me. God was teaching me, through this precious bird, that I needed a change in attitude and perspective. How dark and tense this world would be if all the creatures in it had the same attitude I carried. How different *I* would be if *I* took the time to pause after the completion of each task to rejoice over it, and to thank God for His help. How easily this little bird could have been anxious and troubled—fearful that she could not find the right size of sticks or get them to fit just right. Perhaps she could have been afraid of being an inadequate nest-builder, an inept mother, or a poor singer! And she had so many sticks to get, how could she ever find enough of them in time? She had little ones on the way, already! And then there would be all those mouths to feed. And what about predators?

Fortunately, she didn't appear troubled with all those worries. She didn't even get discouraged about how plain or ugly her nest appeared in comparison to other nests. She simply addressed herself to the task at hand, pausing at the completion of each one to praise the Creator, thereby gladdening the hearts of all who heard her.

The Perfect Attitude

I had to smile as I contrasted her attitude and mine. I really had no reason to allow my mind to be singing a dirge, anyway. While I *imagined* how disappointed everyone must be in this pale replacement of their "perfect" pastor's wife, I had not actually felt rejection from anyone! There were plenty of delightful things about our new district—the motherly love I felt from Louise, the encouragement Pat and Mary Ann exuded, the friendship from Kim, Dorma, Becky, Debbie, Lori, Kathy, and so many others, the lively children, the beauty of our surroundings, the joy I felt with each new request for Bible studies, and the evidence that was slowly unfolding that God was caring for me just as He cared for this lowly catbird in my Rose of Sharon.

One corner of my mouth twitched. Then both corners lifted. I felt the corners of my eyes begin to wrinkle. I was smiling! I resolved to do my little chores, one at a time, and trust the bigger picture to God. Oh, yes, and I must sing!—not just as an assignment—I must choose happy songs to beautify the atmosphere of my home. Into my heart came the desire to have a word in season—or a song in season—for the weary.

Such Sweet Songs

Melody of Praise

*The melody of praise is the atmosphere of heaven;
and when heaven comes in touch with the earth,
there is music and song—
"thanksgiving and the voice of melody"* (Isaiah 52:3).

—Ellen G. White

Now, twenty-some years later, my health, as my outlook, has steadily improved. Some experiences have been joyful, and some very difficult. But through the years I have often reflected on that sweet little catbird and reviewed her lessons. Each time I think about that little mother bird, it leads me once again to renew that step up. Each step is like adding one more stick to the nest. Over time, some of the things I learned from Mrs. Catbird have become clearer. I had so much to learn. I needed to truly trust that God really would help me, even with all my inadequacies. I needed to stop looking at myself and my weaknesses, and I needed to take time many times a day to thank God for each step he helped me with that day.

The Perfect Home

One step at a time, (one stick at a time), God was bringing healing to my heart. He gave me practical help through many avenues, through friends that encouraged me, through a website (http://1ref.us/my) that taught me more about how to organize my time (one fifteen-minute chore at a time, one baby step at a time). He taught me through my husband who bent my mind by telling me, "Yes, Isabelle, you have that problem, but that's not all there is to you!" Another friend blessed me deeply by saying, "Don't be so intimidated, Isabelle, stand tall, even in your messy house!"

How strengthening it was to recognize that this problem needed to be kept in perspective rather than allowing it to destroy every shred of my self-worth. God taught me in the quiet hours to forgive and receive His peace. He taught me to keep on step after step, even if I failed. He taught me to rejoice in small victories. He taught me to look more often at the positives instead of the negatives when the positives seemed small or even insignificant.

In fact, God has been teaching me one day at a time, one step at a time. One day He gave me a special promise in Jeremiah 31:4, "Again I will build thee and thou shalt be built O virgin of Israel... ." Aha! So it's not just about a catbird building a nest, and it's not just about me "building" a home—or a life! No, now the picture has changed. That wise bird also represented God, my Heavenly Father, who has taken on the challenge of re-building *me*. If the catbird's lesson follows through in every single way that He teaches me something new, or builds something new in my life, He too must sing for joy. Is that what it means in Zephaniah 3:17; *The LORD thy God in the midst of thee is mighty; he will save, he will rejoice over thee with joy; he will rest in his love, he will joy over thee with singing*"?

The Perfect Message

Today I take time to thank a busy little catbird in my Rose of Sharon. "Dear little bird, I heard your message that bright spring morning long ago, but not so far away, and I haven't forgotten. Your melody was a gift to me. You told me to keep a song in my heart as I do the duty that lies nearest. It works! It may well be that I owe you not only my happiness, but my very life! Thank you so much!"

---

*pseudonyms

Cleaning Concepts

1. **Awakening:** Put a theme song in your heart as you connect with your Creator; dress in practical clothing, comb hair, brush teeth, make bed, and find a smile.
2. **Kitchen:** Clean the sink, wash, and store dishes. De-clutter countertops for five minutes.
3. **Office:** Begin with the desk and work outward to file papers before they are lost. File folders and filing cabinets are great stress relievers and save searching time.
4. **Bathroom:** Tub and toilet can be sparkling and mold free with a swish and a swipe. Use cabinets, drawers, and shelves to put clutter out of sight. Keep a bucket of cleaning aids handy. Recycle extras.
5. **Livingroom:** If company is coming it's OK to push the clutter into a box to create a suddenly tidy environment. It's a wonderful morale booster, but when ignored for a day or two, those items become chronic clutter.
6. **Develop routines:** Create simple morning and evening routines that include quick clean-ups. Have a routine for departure and arrival (such as the keeping of keys), a weekly and monthly cleaning schedule.
7. **Declutter with little steps:** Break tasks into short steps; fifteen minutes per task is enough. Clean for a few minutes every day. Keep a thrift store donation bag handy; share even some of your favorite knick-knacks. Focus on completely beautifying one room a week.
8. **Accept help:** Be kind and forgiving to clutterers, but make them accountable. Ask for and accept help keeping the house clean; even if a job is not accomplished perfectly, it is still a blessing.

Like the catbird, celebrate your accomplishments, one stick—one song—at a time.

Sir Winston

The wolf and the lamb shall feed together,
and the lion shall eat straw like the bullock…
They shall not hurt nor destroy in all my holy mountain,
saith the LORD.

—Isaiah 65:24, 25

The robin had been my favorite bird since early childhood; that brilliant breast, those smooth and beautifully colored eggs, the ability to hear a worm and dance toward it. In memory, I can put myself right back to that day in Grandma's kitchen when I inhaled the fragrance of my first-grade box of crayons and Mr. Robin became the subject of my earliest recognizable drawing.

Now, these many years later, because of one very special experience, my ear was tuned more keenly to his song. Finally it came, with the melody of praise that I'd been anticipating. Wrapping myself in a thick robe against the early morning chill, I made my way to the office window. There, high in an aspen with the early light of dawn playing across his breast, was the first robin to brave his springtime flight into our little corner of the Peace Country. I smiled, hoping it was Winston…he'd had such a slim chance of survival… it was June 24…

Rufus' Treasure

"Woof!" Rufus' deep bark interrupted my chores. Our big, black Newfoundland-Lab rarely barks except when large wild animals pass through his territory. I could tell he was excited. At the time, I was hanging the last load of clothes.

"What is it Rufus?" I called, tossing a couple of dishtowels and a handful of clothespins into the laundry basket. As I rounded the corner of the house, I did not encounter the large animal I expected (such as the moose that had torn out our garden fence the previous summer), but Rufus appeared to be holding something in his mouth.

"Ru, give!" I commanded. Reluctantly, he dropped a slimy ball of fuzz onto the grass. The baby robin was a little worse for the wear, but alive. I glanced up at the nest perched atop the large supporting log at the northwest corner of our back porch. The chick's mother repeated her alarm call from the nearby apple tree as I reached for her little one. There was considerable damage: a hole in the chick's abdomen, a bloody right wing—possibly broken, and a badly twisted toe.

First Aid

Taking the chick into the house, I poured hydrogen peroxide into his puncture wound and over the torn wing. The shoulder of his wing was bare of scapular feathers. I hoped it was not broken, but I bound it to his torso just in case. His toe injury prevented him from being able to support himself, so I rigged up a splint to hold his "folded toe" straight. After a day of hobbling, he was able to walk.

Because of his indomitable spirit in the face of unlikely odds, we knighted him, Sir Winston. Within hours, he had assumed command of the house. He trained his kitchen crew to keep him full of worms so as to be spared his demeaning lectures. The medical crew had reached the verdict that there appeared to be no internal injuries since "everything was working." The cleaning squad had become proficient at placing paper towels in his favorite perching locations.

Within a week, when the splint was removed, his crooked toe was functioning perfectly. The abdominal wound was healing, and he was moving his wing a little to aid him in balance.

Winston's Kingdom

Little Winston began his day quite early by chirping loudly every few minutes until I released him from his basket in our guest room. As soon as he was released, he hopped happily wherever he wanted to go in his indoor kingdom. He liked the back of the couch and was soon able to take flutter-falls from there to the floor.

Very early he demonstrated an affinity for water. He drank greedily from an eyedropper from the first day of his rehabilitation. Then he learned to associate the sound of running water with playtime. When I turned on the kitchen faucet in the morning, he would hop into the kitchen and look up at me expectantly. I would adjust the stream and lift him to the sink. The first few days he merely satisfied his thirst. Then for a couple of days, he "shampooed" his head. Then he let it drizzle over his shoulders and back. Then, when I placed a plug in the sink, he jumped down and splashed for a minute or two, bathing his entire body. The couch was a good place to dry off and then take a nap.

When his toe and wing were both functioning, Winston would head upstairs at sundown in search of the highest perch in his domain. His bed was a laundry basket lined with rags, paper towels, and tissues so that it could be easily cleaned. His little "bedroom," covered with a cardboard box, resided on the top bunk in the spare bedroom upstairs. He seemed quite content with the arrangement, until about 5:30 am when it was time for breakfast. If I was not already awake by the time, he would begin his wake-up call. I wondered how a mother robin so faithfully keeps her nestlings fed … What patience and energy they have! I've seen adult youngsters perfectly capable of feeding themselves, still demanding parental attention. It must be a love language.

Finding Food

When worms were not readily available, Winston dined on small bits of apple, boiled egg, and bread crumbs. He was very willing to eat spaghetti—to him it must have looked like very long worms!

While Winston was still very young, he accompanied me to the greenhouse for morning watering chores. Regardless of how much breakfast I had fed him, his meals lasted less than an hour. I was often not finished watering by the time he was chirping for food again, so I was obliged to stop and search for bugs if I did not have his food with me.

There are dead flies on the south end of the greenhouse ... why not feed Winston some of those? It was a good solution, or so I thought. I quickly scooped a few "crispy critters" from a cross-support and returned to the grow box where Winston was resting in the shade of a tomato bush, chirping to remind me that he was still waiting for food, but he would not open his beak. I pried his beak open with my thumbnail and attempted to convince him that he would just have to make do with these dehydrated samples. No sooner had those dead flies touched his tongue than he spat them out with contempt and chirped a severe reprimand. I had just flunked "Nestling Food 101."

What to do...? Winston needed something to eat, but he was particular. I was experimenting with a variety of cascading peas which were maturing nicely in several hanging baskets. Would he like those? I squeezed one little fresh pea into his open beak. That hit the spot! I was back in his good graces. After devouring about two dozen peas, he was happy to explore the grow beds while I finished watering.

When I had finished in the greenhouse, I rested in my little prayer garden behind the greenhouse. When I saw some ants and other bugs crawling along the rockery, it occurred to me that it might be time for Winston to begin seeking his own food. For a minute, he hopped along the rock-lined border, paying no heed to the abundance of living food in his vicinity. Then he suddenly stopped and cocked his head as if listening for worms, just like an adult robin. For a few seconds his eyes followed an ant that was approaching his foot. As the ant came within striking range, Winston scooped it up and looked up at me as if to say, "Hey, I can do this myself!" He ate several ants, then tried a different kind of insect that must not have tasted quite as good. He quickly spit it out. For a helpless little orphan, he was surely particular!

Though he still preferred eating from our hands, Winston had graduated! I'd have to think on a proper gift.

The day Winston fed himself for the first time.

Then he learned to pull worms by following behind us as we weeded.

The Legend of Pipi-chu

Except for Harriet's timely visit to encourage Winston's independence, we might still be coddling him. She came to pick up a few hanging baskets from our greenhouse as graduation gifts to her students on the First Nations reserve. When she reached out, Winston hopped onto her hand.

"Pipi-chu!" she chirped. "That's the Cree word for *robin*," she explained. While we finished eating lunch, Harriet shared an ancient native legend.

"Once upon a time, long ago and far away, the three-year-old daughter of the tribal chief wandered into the woods and became lost. It was not yet the time of the big snows, but there were very few leaves left on the trees and the nights were turning cold. The little girl's parents and friends searched for the girl all night. By the next day, everyone was involved in the search as it spread farther and farther into the woods.

During the afternoon of the second day, an elder noticed the strange behavior of the robins flying above him with something in their beaks. His curiosity compelled him to divert from the search long enough to investigate. He followed the line of robins deeper into the woods and saw them drop the contents of their beaks onto a mound at the foot of a tall tree. The elder watched in surprise as many robins added their contributions. As he moved closer, he was able to detect that the robins were dropping leaves on the mound. The leaves were covering a small depression in the earth.

The elder was compelled to explore beneath the leaves. His hand encountered something warm and soft. His heart beating like a tom-tom, he feverishly scooped away the leaves. There she was—the little princess—warm, dry, and fast asleep! What great rejoicing there was around the fire that night while the tribe attempted to explain the actions of the robins. And, though no one has ever really been able to explain it, the Cree Nation has handed down through many generations what has become known as the "Legend of Pipi-chu." Harriett felt honored that Winston chose to sit with her, for she had grown up with high regard for the "sacred bird."

"There is a problem, Linda," Harriett warned. "Unless Winston is able to reintegrate with his own kind, he will not fly south for the winter with them." She went on to explain the problems that her friends had faced when they raised some Canadian geese. I wondered if we were actually doing Winston a favor by saving his life, if he was to be lost to the icy clutch of winter in a few months.

Learning to Fly

Even as a wounded chick, Winston was strong in spirit. At first he was unable to use his wing. I moved it gently to keep it supple. When the wound healed, he began propelling himself with a windmill action and was soon able to jump up to his favorite perch on the back of the couch. When I was reasonably sure that he could fly out of reach of Rufus' jaws, I took him outside to perch in an apple tree and then I returned to the house. When I went back outside a few minutes later, he flew to me and landed

Sir Winston

on my head. He had no fear, and no recollection of the manner in which his near-fatal wounds were inflicted. If he did, he held no grudges. That included Rufus.

When Winston was outside, we kept Rufus indoors so as to provide him a safe environment while he explored his expanding world.

Should we be teaching Winston to fear us? What would strangers do if he landed on their four-wheelers as he did on ours? It was delightful to see him flying, but what is liberty without boundaries?

Winston Disappears

During one town trip, we left Winston inside the house and Rufus outside. When we returned after 7:00 pm, Winston was nowhere to be found. We looked under and around every piece of furniture, called his name repeatedly, opened the refrigerator (not because we thought he might be inside, but because he might come running for a bite to eat), but no little robin came soaring into the kitchen for a supper treat.

My heart sank. Winston was gone. I envisioned him tangled in a cord, crushed in a forgotten mousetrap, upside-down behind a cabinet, suffering or dead in some modern ambush from which I should have protected him. I had hoped that when it was time to roost he would perch on his familiar basket on the bunk bed in the guest room, but he was not there. Where could he be? We dropped to our knees in prayer before going to bed, but sleep did not come easily.

I awoke with a start at 5:30 the next morning, having dreamed that I had heard Winston's tell-tale, wake-up chirp! Was I dreaming, or had I really heard our friendly alarm clock? I willed my breath to come softly—as soft as the down of a newborn chick, lest the sound of my breathing prevent me from hearing the sound in case it was repeated.

I had nearly fallen back to sleep when I heard it. "Chirp!"

I popped out of bed, and ran downstairs, my hope renewed. I was not dreaming. Again the single chirp sounded, but where was it coming from?

Nowhere. Everywhere. It was such a simple song, but my faith was revived; it hung suspended from an invisible strand of hope.

"Chirp!"

I positioned myself at the bottom of the stairs—the crossroad—between up and down, right and left, hope and despair. Maybe you've been there? Afraid to anticipate, armed against disappointment, but still clinging fiercely to a single, fragile evidence of hope. Was this faith or presumption?

"Chirp!"

He sounds healthy! But where is he? Maybe I'm standing in the wrong place. Upstairs? Winston's room? But we've inspected his bedroom so thoroughly…

I had barely opened his door when he proclaimed his joy, and hunger. Still, I could not see him! I looked under the bed, in his basket, in the closet; rechecked the windowsill…

"Chirp-chirp-chirp," he sang, obviously excited. The sound seemed to be coming from…the wall? I pulled a pillow away from the headboard. There he was, perched 'way down on a rod of the antique iron bedstead! I reached my hand down to him, and he willingly jumped onto my finger, totally unaware of the crisis he had caused. He had simply gone to bed on time, and no amount of hollering on our part could rouse him from his peaceful slumber. I sat down on the guest bed, smiling and slowly shaking my head with relief while he shared his dreams and peered out his window. His healthy appetite, a hearty dose of egg-food and a few drops of water, affirmed what had been a restful night—for him, anyway.

In spite of what might be classed as a traumatic beginning, Winston had adapted to his new life; he knew where he belonged, and when his family was not home to "tuck him in," he had located his room, and found a "limb" on which to wrap his feet. He had no "worry box" in which to store a "poor me" from the past; a present "Oh no! Whatever shall I do?" nor a future "What if?" For Winston, bygones were bygones. He lived each day to the fullest, with no regrets. But I began to wonder, after Harriet's warning, was he too trusting?

Sir Winston

Winston's Work Program

Winston's days were full of work and wonder. Though he seemed much better at the wondering, he sometimes took two classes at a time. Here its "Outdoor Bathing and Worms 101."

Can you find Winston in the garden?

Winston always liked "helping" me hang out the clothes, though his "blessings" sometimes required certain articles to endure another wash cycle. The clothesline was a perfect "training perch." It perfectly fit his feet, like a tree limb, even swaying a bit. He "helped" groom hanging baskets... and play the piano.

Bright Spot in Life's Tapestry

I prefer a pastel world—an environment void of confrontations, disappointments, or even the occasional application of much-needed discipline. However, there is less chance that my lessons will need to be repeated if they come to me in bold, high contrast colors. The tapestry of life is

Sir Winston

not designed according to our preferences, but our need. As helpless as Winston was, I needed the lessons he shared more than he needed what I could give him.

The little tyke had been such a bright spot that I could not help but smile at each little reminder of his whole-hearted zest for life. It was as if I could hear his proverbial commands in the demanding chirps he delivered.

- Be patient; healing will come.
- Look up; expect something good.
- Keep climbing; your wings will start working one of these days.
- Be forgiving; don't hold a grudge.
- Enjoy life; there are unexpected gardens growing everywhere.

God used my pain for your good.
—Genesis 50:20 (Winston's Paraphrased Version).

Such Sweet Songs

You are probably able to hurdle the obstacles placed in your pathway of life much more readily than I can overcome mine. I applaud your bravery. I wonder if you, like me, dreamed about someday having a beautiful garden arranged more perfectly than anything you have ever seen; a garden without thorns or weeds where the blossoms never fade, and where the birds will always be singing for there will be no darkness. At all. Ever.

How would you personalize your garden of paradise so as to more perfectly reflect the memory of an important lesson? Oh?—You'd like to add an arbor of climbing roses to commemorate a dark tunnel through which you developed your sweet song of faith? Me?...Yes ... a bird bath I think... .

Winston had only taken a few dips in his graduation gift when he disappeared. I freshened his birdbath daily hoping that he would return for a short conversation, and we all kept a close eye out for him while driving our quads, but, though there was one robin who seemed much less afraid of us, who sat on a certain post when we weeded the garden, and took a shower each time we turned on the sprinkler, the baby Winston who'd been so dependent on us did not return.

I listen closely for the return of the robins each spring. Above all the other gifts he imparted, Winston gave me an ear to hear.

Sir Winston

Hearing His Voice

*Children should be encouraged to search out in nature
the objects that illustrate Bible teachings,
and to trace in the Bible the similitudes drawn from nature.
They should search out, both in nature and in Holy Writ,
every object representing Christ,
and those also that He employed in illustrating truth… .
They may learn to hear His voice in the song of birds,
in the sighing of the trees, in the rolling thunder,
and in the music of the sea.*

—Ellen G. White

Service

You never hear the robins boast about the sweetness of their song,
Nor do they stop their music gay whene'er a poor man comes along.
God taught them how to sing an' when they'd
learned the art He sent them here
To use their talents day by day the dreary lives o' men to cheer
An' rich or poor an' sad or gay, the ugly an' the fair to see,
Can stop most anytime in June an' hear the robins' melody.

I stand an' watch them in the sun, usin' their gifts from day to day,
Swellin' their little throats with song, regardless of men's praise or pay;
Jes' bein' robins, nothing else, nor claiming greatness for their deeds,
But jes' content to gratify one of the big world's many needs,
Singin' a lesson to us all to be ourselves an' scatter cheer
By usin' every day the gifts God gave us when He sent us here.

Why should we keep our talents hid, or think we favor men because
We use the gifts that God has given? The robins never ask applause,
Nor count themselves remarkable, nor strut in a superior way,
Because their music sweeter is than that God gave unto the jay.
Only a man conceited grows as he makes use of talents fine,
Forgetting that he merely does the working of the Will Divine.

Lord, as the robins, let me serve! Teach me to do the best I can
To make this world a better place, an' happier for my fellow man.
If gift o' mine can cheer his soul and hearten him along his way
Let me not keep that talent hid; I would make use of it today.
An' since the robins ask no praise, or pay for all their songs o' cheer,
Let me in humbleness rejoice to do my bit o' service here.

—*Edgar A. Guest*

Bluebird in My Path

—Cheri Peters

For the invisible things of him from the creation of the world are clearly seen, being understood by the things that are made, [even] his eternal power and Godhead; so that they are without excuse…

—Romans 1:20

This story first appeared in Cheri Peter's book, <u>A Miracle from the Streets</u>.* When I contacted her about including her bluebird encounter, she kindly gave me permission to include the amazing story in this volume—another story of how God can speak to the listening ear.

"Donna, can we take another walk? I'm overwhelmed even talking about those two weeks. The pictures are too vivid. I'm scared."

Donna stood and reached out her hand to pull me out of my chair. But even more than her physical assistance and love was her warm grip that was lifting me up and out of my past. She couldn't fully realize how much her friendship meant to me.

Shadows haunted the edges of the trail as we once more walked the path among the tall pines. I went through the motions of trying to relax, but my mind was far from restful.

What was that? Was someone behind that tree?

I just knew that a biker** would jump out from behind a tree and tear me to pieces. The forest that had so invigorated me just hours before, now filled me with fright. My breath came in short, shallow gasps.

Walking over to a fallen tree, I sat down on the sagging bark, lost in my thoughts, trying to get my bearings.

God, please make Yourself real to me. I need to know that You are here. I need to be safe for once. I want so much to know that You are real, that You love me.

How can you really love me with this trail of garbage in my life? And how can I ever hope to be normal? I don't even know how to act in any situation unless I am drugged. I have nothing of value that I do or that I know. I have only done what I thought those around me expected of me my whole life in order to survive. Oh God, I am so worthless!

A beautiful bluebird fluttered to a branch within a few feet of where I sat. The thin branch quivered and bounced as she ruffled her feathers, beginning to preen. I could have reached out and touched her!

Why isn't she afraid of me?

The answer landed in my heart as quickly and softly as the bird herself; she was not afraid because God was taking care of her. God was keeping her safe.

And I will keep you safe, too, Cheri.

God will keep me safe! A burst of joy filled me. I wanted to leap from the trunk and whoop, but the bird was still there. I didn't want to scare her away.

Is the voice that I just heard a silly notion? No.

I was too afraid to ask Donna, for fear of marring my new friendship, but I knew my experience was real.

I breathed deeply of the fresh forest air, filling every space possible in my lungs. The air was fresh, the shadows playful. The forest was beautiful again. The bird stretched her wings. In a swoop of feather and a soft note cheer, she was gone.

Bluebird in My Path

Goodbye bluebird! Thank you! Dear God, do You use nature to teach us about You? Of course You do! You just did!

"God has given us so much," Donna said, almost to herself. "All we have to do is accept it!" She was sitting on a lichen-covered stone, breathing in the beauty of the language of Nature with which she had become familiar.

Were eyes being opened and my ears unstopped? Warmth flooded my inmost soul, and I desperately desired to learn the language of heaven that began with an assurance delivered to me by a tiny blue messenger, a silent but overwhelming conviction, right when I needed it.

I am safe!

---

*Order Cheri's book, *Miracle from the Streets*, from her website: http://1ref.us/mx

**Member of the Hell's Angels gang from which Cheri had recently escaped

Joyful Trust

The birds are teachers of the sweet lesson of trust.
Our heavenly Father provides for them;
but they must gather the food,
they must build their nests and rear their young.
Every moment they are exposed to enemies
that seek to destroy them.
Yet how cheerily they go about their work!
How full of joy are their little songs!

—Ellen G. White

Mourning Lullaby

—Darlene Willard

Blessed are they that mourn: for they shall be comforted.

—Matthew 5:4

For the past four years, my long-time friend, Darlene Willard, has been keeping me updated on a very meaningful relationship she has formed with a wild mourning dove that she calls Baby. It has been during this time that she and her husband, Bob, have had a series of heartaches and unbelievable close calls, one after the other. Through it all, Baby's presence has been an uplifting influence, and her yearly returns have become something which they anticipate with joy.

"Mom and Dad, it's the very place for you," our eldest son concluded his phone call with such enthusiasm that Bob and I couldn't help but believe Rob's report about the little piece of heaven he'd discovered 'way out in Wyoming. "It's not far from a little country town. The place isn't fancy. It's not like anywhere you've lived before. It's quiet and restful, with plenty of elbow room, and good country neighbors, an abundance of water and good agricultural land. I can see you finally being able to spend some time creating the beautiful flower gardens that you so much enjoy. I just know you'll love it! How soon can you come?"

When we saw "the place," we felt God had influenced Rob in finding it. His retirement gift has helped ease the pain of the unexpected hurdles of our golden years in a way we could never have anticipated. How could we have known that our beautiful *Willard Gardens*, as we named our new home, came with its very own angel? How can we express our gratitude for her divinely-timed appointments except to share the story?

Willard Gardens

It was during the spring of 2013 that a pair of mourning doves (*Zenaida macroura*, also called turtle doves) favored us with their presence. They announced their arrival softly. If I hadn't loved and communicated with animals since my early childhood, I may not have noticed them. They blended so artistically with the little Eden that we were attempting to create that it seemed they completed the picture.

As the days passed I noticed that the doves seemed more attentive if I was alone. They directed their calls to me from the telephone wires, tree branches, and the roof of our house. Swooping low, barely over my head, they tried to get my attention if I did not respond to their conversational advances. They were not pests, but they seemed to have a real desire to communicate. When I acknowledged them, they would sing to me, eat a few seeds, and then fly away until their next visit. They deserved names; I called them Pretty Boy and Baby.

Eventually, when I would walk toward the house at the close of my workday, both doves would begin screeching in a raucous tone, so different from their sweet cooing, as if to say, "Don't leave! Don't leave! Don't go in the house, yet! It's not even dark!"

"I'll see you tomorrow," I would assure them as I closed the door.

As the summer wore on, the doves came ever nearer as I continued to shape the garden designs that Bob and I had envisioned. Although we were officially retired, Bob had accepted a part time custodial position, leaving me to play in the gardens. On these days, the doves would come very close to me, pecking at bugs and seeds, and taking a bath in the shallow ponds that Bob had constructed. Cocking their little heads, they would chirp cheerfully in my direction, waiting for my response, as if wondering whether I had learned their language yet. Their friendship energized me, and their songs were inspirational. I wished I knew their words.

Animal Talk

Early in life, I fell in love with animals. They understood me, and I understood them. Fortunately, Bob also loved animals, or he might have at least raised his eyebrows when I attempted to speak Dove. Our doves were not just birds—they seemed eager to understand our efforts to beautify their yard.

Though the two doves might look identical to a casual observer, I could easily tell them apart; Pretty Boy had a faint, dark necklace around his neck. Baby had the same continuous color, and there was no mistaking her clever, animated personality. Pretty Boy and Baby were attentive to each other, but they never did nest, so I wondered if they were actually a pair.

Our dogs, Jon Pierre and Katrina, took it upon themselves to protect the doves from other wildlife, including wild rabbits and birds who frequented our three ponds. It was as if the dogs understood that the doves needed their guardianship. They were never jealous of our attentions to the doves.

There was no doubt that the doves felt accepted. They roused me early every morning. It became common for my dear husband, Bob, to awaken me with a tap on my shoulder. "Honey, your friends are calling you from the telephone wire!" It was as if they were awaiting my "call-back." I would rouse myself, climb upstairs, poke my head out of the upstairs window and carry on my first conversation of the day. They listened and replied cheerfully, acknowledging, if not understanding, my words.

Lest someone think I might be exaggerating their attachment for us, I'll tell about the day Baby and Pretty Boy followed us into town. It was time to leave for church one bright Sabbath morning. The doves watched us as we loaded our food box. We looked up at them, waved, said goodbye, and hopped into our car. Fifteen miles later, when we parked in the church parking lot in Torrington, the two of them swooped in and perched on a branch directly above us! Baby went through her now-familiar song-and-dance ritual, obviously pleased with their little trick!

It took awhile for me to actually get into the church building that morning. I just couldn't leave those two birds after they had demonstrated such loyalty! I took time to thank them and ask God to protect them. I slowly walked toward the building, glancing back several times. They were still on the branch watching me. I would have liked to invite them inside. They were at home waiting for us, on the wire directly above the driveway, when we drove back home that afternoon.

Good News, Bad News

When our doves left for the winter, I missed them. Their song was such a soft and tender gift to us. Had I taken their presence too much for granted? Would they return in the spring? Would I ever hear their sweet-sorrowful song again? I prayed for them all winter, pleading that God would spare their lives and return them safely to us.

One morning, early in April of 2014, I heard a familiar, and very anticipated, song. I hurried outside. Baby was back! There was no mistaking her antics and friendly manner. Hand in hand, Bob and I anxiously scanned the sky for Pretty Boy, but he never returned. If Baby was lonely, I couldn't detect it. She continued her regular pattern of awakening me, morning by morning, with her gentle cooing, and following me around the yard throughout the day.

A few weeks later, June 14, 2014, our precious Rob died very unexpectedly of a heart attack the day before Father's Day. Little did we know that this healthy appearing, very athletic young man had any health problems! His death was totally unexpected; I felt as if I had been punched in the stomach and couldn't catch my breath. Just the week before his death, he and his brother, Greg, had taken Bob for a weekend outing to Yellowstone Park, a short drive from our home. My men had not been together on a special trip by themselves since the boys had left home. It was a sentimental and very meaningful trip for Dad and his sons.

The morning before he passed away, Rob had called to tell me all the latest happenings in his life. Before he hung up, he assured me, three times, of his love.

"I love you, Mamma!" he said cheerfully. "Tell Dad I'll be calling him on Father's Day!" But, there was no call. We would never hear that beloved voice again. It was as if a candle had been snuffed out and we were left in darkness. How could we cope? God prepared a way.

In mid-summer, another male dove began to accompany Baby. Though he never became as friendly to us as Pretty Boy had been, those dear little birds brought us great comfort. Their happy songs and antics helped us smile in spite of our grief. Bob and I both considered them a gift from our Heavenly Father, reminding us of the presence of the heavenly dove, The Comforter, Himself. Then came the onset of winter, and our sweet singers were gone. It was a long winter. Again, I prayed for their safe return.

As December 2014 approached, Bob's anxiety increased. Rob's death, and other heartaches within our family, left him so deeply sorrowful that I sometimes feared for his life; his intense anguish simply had to escape. Before long, he developed a severe case of shingles. The sores were situated along the nerve located directly over his heart. He had unexplained phantom pains, which put us in the emergency room of the hospital in Torrington for extensive medical tests. Although all of his blood tests were negative for heart damage, he returned home weak and unable to work because of his continued heart pain. I was in despair over seeing my precious Prince so miserable.

In response to my e-mail asking for spiritual support during this battle, friends and family across the US and Canada began praying. Within two months Bob was completely recovered—an unheard-of time frame for such a severe case. In fact, his doctor told him that he considered Bob's healing an absolute miracle! It was a gift, a very necessary gift, for within a month it would be Bob who was helping me through a medical dilemma with my own heart.

In January 2015, I had to undergo a totally unexpected open heart surgery: two bypasses and a new aortic valve. Life changed considerably. Following my operation, I was not able to participate in my outdoor activities as energetically as usual, nor converse as often with Baby. She seemed to miss me.

Weather Watcher

One July morning, Baby called and called, incessantly. Still in recovery, I slowly made my way to the door, and stood leaning on the door frame listening to her chatter excitedly. I spoke to her, and she returned my greeting, but it also seemed she was trying to deliver a more urgent message. She almost danced on the electric wire, going through all sorts of antics to get my attention. I wished I knew what she was trying to say to me before she disappeared. When we listened to the weather station on television, we learned that we were to have a heavy hailstorm and high winds. Upon hearing the weather warning in our own language, we became concerned for her safety, and began praying for her and her wild friends. Does not God put instincts within the heart of wild creatures? Do they have premonitions and try to warn us?

The horrible storm finally subsided, leaving much damage in its wake. Was Baby alright? After assessing garden damage, we had just seated ourselves down to a late breakfast when we heard the familiar soft cooing of our friend just outside the window. What welcomed music!

As quickly as my compromised health would allow, I shuffled out to acknowledge our little angel. I discovered her on the telephone line at the front of the house, looking down expectantly, answering my joyful greeting of what I hoped was appropriate vocabulary (how does one talk to a dove, anyway?). Baby was safely home once again. Bob and I bowed together to thank our Heavenly Father for His protection of our home, and our harbinger of joy. As she flew away, my heart went with her.

The Lullaby

I arose much earlier than usual on the first anniversary of Rob's death. Weighed down with grief, sleep had not come to me. It was still dark when I sought the comfort of my old rocking chair where I am accustomed to start each day. On my way upstairs, I lifted the pretty green container with Rob's ashes from the mantle. Cradling the precious urn in my arms, I slowly climbed the staircase and collapsed in my chair. In silent desperation, I kept rocking—unanswered questions burning through my troubled mind. How do people set their life in order after a tragedy? How can I begin to cope with this grief? Will I ever be able to cry? Where can I find relief?

I don't know how long I sat there aching and rocking and praying with no relief of my sorrow, but my sadness was unexpectedly lifted, by a soft, sweet sound coming from over my right shoulder. Opening my eyes, I turned my head and there was my little Baby, brightened by the early morning sunlight, sitting on the sill of the open window nearest my rocking chair. She was looking right at me, singing with her head cocked a little to one side, as if intent on communicating her message to me. It was as if she, too, knew what mourning meant (could she still remember Pretty Boy?) and that she had learned the words to her gentle lullaby in the school of sorrow, herself. On wings of song, Baby wedged her comforting message into the very place where my heart was hurting.

Although Baby generally called to us from near our downstairs bedroom window every morning, this is the one and only time she has ever sat on a windowsill of our home. That morning she was as close as she could get to where I was sitting and still remain outside. It was as though God, empathizing with my depth of sorrow, placed her there for my comfort. In that moment, I appreciated the depth of my Father's love as never before.

Such Sweet Songs

"Oh Baby!" I sighed, in deep gratitude. "He sent you to comfort me! Thank you for caring!" My little dove answered with a gentle murmur and stayed there on the bright windowsill, singing her sweet lullaby of peace to me for several minutes before rising upward and disappearing into a sunbeam.

My burden eased. Knowing that God truly understood my sorrow, I began to praise Him for life, for loaning me such a wonderful son and loving husband! I thanked him for Baby and her comforting lullaby. Gratefulness bubbled up, uncontrollably, from that very same place in my heart where I had been experiencing such unbearable pain before Baby delivered her healing melody. I knew that God had something special in store for Bob's healing journey, too.

Cradlesong

In the past few weeks, Bob had withdrawn socially. I knew it was because of grief, but how could I help him? I'd been overwhelmed with my own anguish. Breaking open our silent sorrow that morning, Bob and I shared some precious memories about Rob, and then prayed together, mingling our tears, begging God to help us get through this anniversary of our unbearable loss. That experience was the cradlesong of our rebirth. On that lullaby morning, our faith and trust in God was multiplied exponentially.

That day we worked in the portion of our yard that we had set aside as Rob's Memory Garden. That night we both slept like babies. In fact, Bob slept nearly twelve hours without stirring, which is totally out of character for him! By Monday he was his cheerful self, again, determined to get some projects finished. Nestled between the birds and the flowers, Bob and I sensed release from our paralyzing sorrow. Though we have had moments of deep sadness, never again have we suffered the level of desperation that we suffered on that first anniversary of Rob's death. we experienced a freedom and energy that we'd been lacking for weeks.

Does Jesus Care?

Does Jesus care when I've said "goodbye"
To the dearest on earth to me,
And my sad heart aches till it nearly breaks,
Is it aught to Him? Does He see?
Oh yes, He cares, I know He cares,
His heart is touched with my grief;
When the days are weary, the long nights dreary,
I know my Savior cares.

—Frank E. Graeff and J. Lincoln Hall

Does God care? You bet He does! Our ears, dulled with life's painful experiences, cannot always hear Him, but He's there. Sometimes His voice is heard in beauty and song. One component of my healing journey has been to acknowledge His messages of assurance. No matter what I go through, I will never endure it alone. I see His smile in the face of flowers and hear the echoes of His understanding each morning that Baby calls down the chimney to me. I talk to Him with a deeper sense of His presence.

Garden Lesson

After working extra hours in Rob's Memorial Garden and planting several annuals for a riot of summer color, we were just beginning to enjoy the brilliant purple, magenta, and pink petunias when a storm roared through and dumped hail the size of hen's eggs on our yard. It felt as if my heart broke anew when I saw the mess. Every single petunia blossom was shredded—not a trace of color remained.

As the days passed, however, the torn plants struggled back to life and began to bloom again. The storm had so effectively pruned them that they were more luxuriant that summer than they would have been under my (over)protection. And it wasn't just the petunia revival that spoke the heart lesson—the entire garden was more glorious than we had ever seen it!

Somewhere between Rob's garden and Baby's lullaby, my faith grew. Recording my thoughts and then rereading my experience, it was as if I viewed my trial from a higher perspective. One day, I will be able to see the end from the beginning to understand that God has allowed certain things to develop my faith—the faith of those Bible heroes that I love to read about who knew that God was right beside them in every storm.

Something else changed in me, after capturing my story in written form. Bob can see it. I have a profound joy and boundless energy. I feel a deeper empathy with others who have experienced loss, and an ever-deepening appreciation for what my Father suffered—how difficult it was for Him to lose His Perfect Son because of my imperfections.

Why do bad things happen? Can finite beings ever really understand the whole picture? No, but the time I learned to trust Him has been in the dark valleys. Maybe those hard-shelled seeds of faith are only softened in the storm?

What a joy it will be when the Garden of Eden is restored and I will more fully appreciate the results of my storm damage. Once I am safely

Mourning Lullaby

Home, I am sure that I will see that He allowed only as much hail as would help me to accept the design that He desired me to fulfill in His Everlasting Garden. Will I not then understand that I was created for oneness with Him, oneness with all the creatures of His creation?

Will I finally be able to speak proper Dove Talk? I wonder—could I begin now? Baby would like that! She's out in Rob's Memorial Garden waiting to tell me about her morning. She has already taught me one sentence; "There is joy in mourning—eventually." She's such a good teacher.

Resurrection

There's a tender Easter legend—
True or false, ah, who can say?—
How a bird with broken pinion
Dead within the garden lay.
And the children, cruel children,
Lifted it by shattered wing,
Shouting, "Make us merry music!
Sing, you lazy fellow, sing!"
But the Christ-child took it from them
(He alone could understand),
Reaching out with tender mercy,
Lifted it with gentle hand.
Then He whispered to it softly,
Laid His lips upon its throat,
And, the song of life returning—
Sounded forth in one glad note.

—*Anon*

(I captured this poem as my friend Bea Kurjata remembered it from childhood and I have, as yet, been unable to establish its authorship.)

Creation

I never see a butterfly
Or hear a singing bird,
But what in some strange manner I
Am very deeply stirred.

Who first conceived the tender wings
On which it seeks the rose?
Has human thought such lovely things
To fashion and disclose?

O singing bird upon a tree!
Has ever a human mind
Contrived to solve the mystery
Of how you were designed?

Man writes his loftiest thoughts in words,
And builds with brick and stone.
But dreams of butterflies and birds
Belong to God alone.

—*Edgar A. Guest*

Yellow Bird

As a bird that wandereth from her nest,
so is a man that wandereth from his place.

—Proverbs 27:8

There is no more invigorating smell in Canada's far north than cottonwoods in the springtime—there is healing in the leaves. It was just such a fragrant morning in May that the Parker family discovered gold as they prepared to walk to the post office. The gold was not in the stream, in the ground, nor even in a mineshaft. It was in a very unlikely place—a tree! It was as if the Creator Himself had dabbed His celestial brush into some brilliant yellow joy so that the discouraged family would be sure to see it perched jauntily, right there on the limb beside their front door.

As one of my favorite authors, Hannah Hurnard, would say, "To the child of God, there are no second causes." Names are changed; the setting is very real.

A Song in the Woods

"Have you ever seen a bird like that one, Nellie?" Slim asked his wife, as she and his three-year-old daughter stepped into the bright, spring morning to join him for the short walk to the post office.

Such Sweet Songs

Nellie peeked through the freshly emerging leaves to get a better look. "Well, it could be some kind of warbler, but it looks more like…a canary!"

"Me see, too?" begged little Esther.

Nellie hoisted the toddler onto her hip and pointed to the dab of yellow among the trees in their mud-and-snow patched yard. The bird chose that moment to begin singing.

"Oh, Mommy, catch it?" Esther clapped her hands.

"I don't think I can do that, dear," said Nellie, setting the child on the ground. "I'm sure, by his song, that this is a canary. He has probably recently escaped from his owner, but canaries are not easily tamed. Neither will he survive long if the weather turns cold again. Perhaps I should see…"

Holding tightly to her father's hand, little Esther tried to be patient while her mother stepped cautiously toward the bird. The little bird cocked his head at Nellie's approach, but he did not fly away.

"Oh, Mommy!" Esther cried, clasping her hands together to help her resist petting the fragile songster when her mother returned. The foursome entered the cabin where the little yellow bird made himself at home on a curtain rod and seemed to enjoy the warmth.

"Now what, Slim?" Nellie asked, as she stood guard at the wood stove. "He needs some safe housing."

"I'll run over to Girard's Second-Hand Store and see if they have a cage," he said, reaching for the doorknob with his eye on the bird.

"Yes, someone is missing him very much," Nellie nodded.

"Can we keep him, Mommy?" Esther asked as her father closed the cabin door.

"Yes," replied her mother, "but only until we find out who he belongs to, Pumpkin."

Prayer for a Sign

Some hearts are always open to the needy; that's why the Parkers were in the Peace Country. Shortly after their marriage, they had moved to the Peace Country to work among the First Nations people. Slim was not trained as a pastor. Neither he nor Nellie had any professional missionary training, but they had prayed and been guided to this place, at least that is what they thought when they first came to Little Prairie, nestled in the foothills of the Canadian Rockies. Their work had not progressed as they had hoped. Life had not been easy. Funds were tight, and it had been a long, cold winter.

Hanging blankets over the kitchen corner and folding the bedding from the pews on which they slept, the Parker's tiny one-room cabin doubled as a church one day in seven. A few of the native children came to story hour every week, but not one adult had ever stayed to hear the words of encouragement Slim so badly wanted to share with them. It appeared to the Parkers that they had become a baby-sitting service, and they were finding it challenging to remain enthusiastic. Doubts unexpressed hovered between the two of them like a hummingbird looking for a place to land, but for fear of discouraging each other, they had avoided discussing the subject. Just the night before they found the friendly yellow bird, Nellie had finally voiced her concern.

"Slim, do you think we have misunderstood what God wanted us to do?" she asked, smoothing a curl back from her sleeping daughter's damp forehead. Lacking a rocking chair, she always sat beside her daughter after reading the children's Bible story until Esther fell asleep. Then she would wedge a chair beside the pew so that little Esther wouldn't fall off during the night. The silence was neither painful nor peaceful; Nellie and Slim both sensed that it was time for a discussion, maybe even a decision. Slim stoked the cook stove, their only source of heat, and then sat down beside his wife.

"I don't know, Nellie," Slim sighed. "It seemed plain enough when we left Alberta, didn't it?" Slim purposefully brightened when he saw the sad look that passed across his wife's face. "Let's pray again, Sweetheart." With their arms encircling the sleeping form of their little daughter, they knelt together that evening and prayed for evidence of divine guidance. Yes, they had prayed before, but this time they asked for an unmistakable sign.

"Dear Lord, You know why we are here. You know who needs to come. Please send us the souls who need to hear Your Good News. Please send us a direct sign that we are where You want us to be. We want so badly to share Your love. Amen."

The very next morning, there he was—a sign in the tree right outside their door! Or course, Slim and Nellie didn't recognize Yellow Bird as the sign for which they were looking, nevertheless, the adventure had begun. It had actually started two days earlier, just as another young couple were finishing supper in another home not far from Slim and Nellie's cabin.

A New Prayer

Nancy looked across the table at her husband, Bill, knowing she hardly dared broach the subject that had been plaguing her for weeks.

"I really miss going to church," she said, appearing to address her cup of coffee rather than her husband. "I know it would be difficult to find a church family as loving as the folks back home. We're pretty new here…"

Yellow Bird

Tears glistened in her eyes when she finally looked up. "I thought when we got married it would be enough just to have each other, but I really miss the spiritual support."

Bill stirred his cup and placed his spoon in his saucer before he answered, "I have to admit, I really miss the companionship of fellow believers, too, but where would we find a nice church family in this isolated town?" Silence reigned. Then Bill finally asked, "Want to pray about it, Nancy?"

Bill and Nancy joined hands and prayed together for the first time since their move. That's how the story really started—right there, beside the kitchen table with Nancy's beloved pet canary, Yellow Bird, on the curtain rod above them. Was he listening? Bill's prayer went something like this.

"Lord, we're lonely. We need You. Please guide us to a church family who really cares."

"Amen!" Nancy declared.

When she arose from her knees, Nancy opened the sliding glass door to freshen the living room. The cool, evening breeze was laden with the inviting scent of cottonwood, a smell she had loved for as long as she could remember. She stood in the doorway just breathing in the wonderful aroma, and then…

What happened next left Nancy standing with her mouth open, but not in joy. A flash of yellow darted through the door and into the upper limbs of a tall cottonwood. Yellow Bird! Nancy tried to keep the panic out of her voice as she quickly took the empty cage outside and called to her pet, but by the strength of his song, Nancy knew that Yellow Bird was enjoying his perch high in the cottonwood even more than the human hands he'd learned to trust. At last, Yellow Bird was left to fend for himself as best he could.

Nancy didn't sleep much that night. She awakened several times hoping, but afraid to pray, that she would find Yellow Bird in his cage by morning. He wasn't. In fact, he was no longer in the big cottonwood tree, either. She put out some of his favorite foods that day, but he never returned.

Bill tried to comfort Nancy, but the loss of her beloved pet only added to the misery that her heart had been collecting, one grief at a time, since the day they had left Alberta: their family, their friends, and finally, God. Yellow Bird was all Nancy had left of the soft, comfortable memory she once called "home."

All Things Possible

Loneliness settled over Nancy like a shroud. She felt totally abandoned. She recalled why she had decided that she didn't want God in her life—He was always asking the impossible and making life miserable. There had been things she'd wanted to do, freedoms she'd wanted to experience, and although they had turned out to be empty joys, she had enjoyed her sense of freedom since leaving home. The absence of her bird was a punishment, wasn't it? Tears of frustration, rebellion, then overwhelming sadness soaked her pillow. Even Bill's loving words and tender strokes could not warm her heart.

In the midst of the week, after finishing his shift at the mill, Bill stopped at the store, picked up some special treats for Nancy and a copy of the small town's weekly newspaper. Nancy tried to be appreciative of Bill's thoughtfulness, kissing him, but without her usual enthusiasm at his safe return. Her joy had taken flight.

Nancy half-heartedly busied herself with supper preparations. Bill opened his newspaper. Over the top edge of the want ads Bill's eyes automatically focused on the empty, very quiet cage in the far corner of the living room. Yellow Bird's silence was even louder than his song. The cage seemed to symbolize their existence—empty, purposeless, without pleasure.

Bill let the newspaper drop into his lap. He stared at the cage in much the same way he would study a campfire, not exactly focusing, but warming to the memories of good times they had shared with Yellow Bird before they had married and moved to Little Prairie. A smile bubbled up somewhere inside; he hadn't thought he would miss the yellow rocket landing on his head every night when Nancy let him fly free, but he did.

"If I could have just one wish... ." Bill left the sentence unfinished as he turned his attention back to the newspaper. Immediately his eyes fell on a small ad under the "Lost and Found" notices:

FOUND—One Yellow Canary
Claim at the Gospel Tabernacle
North Frontage Road

Bill jumped up, ran to the kitchen and thrust the newspaper in front of his wife, the thrill of hope overwhelming his ability to speak.

"Oh, Bill!" Nancy breathed, her eyes suddenly alight. "Do you think it's possible....?"

She quickly turned off the electric range, Bill grabbed the cage, and they jumped into their old pickup. It didn't take them long to find the Parker's tiny cabin nestled among the aspens. Afraid to hope, they clasped hands as they walked forward, and before they reached the cabin their hope was rewarded with a song they thought they'd never hear again.

When the door opened Bill and Nancy found even more than their golden singer—they discovered a room full of love and the true gold for which they had prayed that very week! It was the beginning of a lifetime of a deep and meaningful friendship.

For Nancy, the revelation of God's goodness overruled her rebellious fears about His ways of doing things. If ever she was tempted to doubt, she would close her eyes and once again see herself walking toward a tiny cabin in the woods, hearing heaven's song of hope.

Sympathy

I know what the caged bird feels, alas!
When the sun is bright on the upland slopes;
When the wind stirs soft through the springing grass,
And the river flows like a stream of glass;
When the first bird sings and the first bud opes,
And the faint perfume from its chalice steals—
I know what the caged bird feels!

I know why the caged bird beats his wing
Till its blood is red on the cruel bars;
For he must fly back to his perch and cling
When he fain would be on the bough a-swing;
And a pain still throbs in the old, old scars
And they pulse again with a keener sting—
I know why he beats his wing!

I know why the caged bird sings, ah me,
When his wing is bruised and his bosom sore,—
When he beats his bars and he would be free;
It is not a carol of joy or glee,
But a prayer that he sends from his heart's deep core,
But a plea, that upward to Heaven he flings—
I know why the caged bird sings!

—Paul Laurence Dunbar (1899)

Song of Peace

*Spring is here, the flowers are in bloom
and the cooing of doves is heard in the land.*

—Song of Solomon 2:12 (Clear Word)

How does a person come to grips with unexpected and unwelcome news? When it's good news, it's not difficult. But, undesirable news is never easy to take. One can too easily forget the details of how they have been led through hard times in the past. Faith is remembering the beauty of past deliverances. When we just can't remember, sometimes we get a little reminder that He is watching, even before the answer comes.

My good friend Barbara and her husband, James, had rented a beautiful country home. After they had gone to much expense and made careful improvements, the landlord suddenly served them a notice of eviction, explaining that he would now be renting the house to a friend of his.

James and Barbara immediately began what proved to be a fruitless search for a country rental located in their vicinity. As the time neared for them to be out of the house, Barbara was tempted to panic. Questions raced through her mind and threatened to drown her in despair. Why did this happen? Where would they move? Was God really watching over them? Did He truly care?

Such Sweet Songs

In an attempt to calm her fears of potential homelessness one bitterly cold winter morning, Barbara sat down to hug a steaming cup of peppermint tea. She inhaled deeply of the enchantingly fresh aroma, successfully preventing the tears of frustration that threatened to salt her brew. At that dark, early morning hour, by faith, she chose to believe that something would work out—in heaven's way, in His time.

It was at the moment, when she considered casting her doubts aside, that she first heard the song. It was not totally unfamiliar, but it was so inappropriate that she couldn't quite place the source of the soft murmuring outside the kitchen window. As the sound intensified, she associated it with springtime. She could almost smell the blossoms...

Barbara didn't usually open the kitchen blinds until the sun was up, but this morning she wanted to identify the soft sounds that were lifting her spirit. Barbara opened the window blind. A pair of mourning doves were looking back at her from a branch of the pine tree that was level with the window. For awhile the doves were silent, but they did not leave. As Barbara returned to her cup of tea, the pair began cooing with renewed vigor.

Photo by Barbara Flees

Song of Peace

Every morning thereafter, the gentle song of the doves reassured Barbara that she was not forgotten. Not long after that encouraging sign appeared, James and Barbara found a new home. Barbara was convinced that the song was a promise of peace in spite of her sorrow, in spite of broken promises when she and James had done their utmost to be model renters.

Perhaps, in the midst of future disappointments, Barbara would recall the song of peace.

The Ark and the Dove

A rain once fell upon the earth
For many a day and night,
And hid the flowers, the grass, the trees,
The birds and beasts, from sight.

The deep waves covered all the land,
And mountain-tops so high;
And nothing could be seen around,
But water, and the sky.

But yet there was one moving thing,
A still and lonely ark,
That, many a weary day and night,
Sailed o'er that ocean dark.

At last, a little dove was forth
From that lone vessel sent;
But, wearied, to the ark again,
When evening came, she bent.

Again she went, but soon returned,
And in her beak was seen
A little twig--an olive-branch
With leaves of shining green.

The waters sank, and then the dove
Flew from the ark once more,
And came not back, but lived among
The tree-tops, as before.

Then from the ark they all came forth,
With songs of joy and praise;
And once again the green earth smiled
Beneath the sun's warm rays.

—H. P. Nichols

I Heard, I Listened

And thine ears shall hear a word behind thee, saying,
This is the way, walk ye in it,
when ye turn to the right hand, and when ye turn to the left.

—Isaiah 30:21

*S*tephanie* *was only fifteen, but her "odometer of life" already had plenty of mileage on it.... She had seen the bad side of family life for many years. Over and over again, she had prayed that her parents could resolve their differences, but it seemed impossible. She was so torn, wanting to please both parents, but it looked as if she was going to have to choose between them. How would she do it? Awake or asleep, the thought plagued her. When the time came, from just outside her window, the answer rang clear as a bell.*

Dad was yelling again. I decided to go down to my older brother's room in the basement and turn up the TV. I ran downstairs, plopped onto the bed, and wrapped a pillow over my head, but that didn't prevent me from hearing my mother call out desperately for help.

"Stephanie!" Mom sounded fearful. "Steph, help!"

I took the stairs three at a time and barged into my parents' bedroom. Dad was roughly pressing Mom down onto the bed. Though I had suspected it earlier, it was the first time I had ever seen Dad physically mistreat Mom.

"Dad," I yelled, trying to get in between the two of them. "Let go of Mom!"

He yanked Mom up and then pushed her down on the bed, again. This time she fell on me.

"I'm calling the police," Dad snarled as he left the room.

When the two policemen arrived, Dad was gone. They questioned each of us, ultimately accusing Mom of abusing Dad! Before they left, they warned her to stop harassing him!

I slept with Mom in her room that night, and though Dad was gone, I felt his presence. Each time I awoke feeling afraid of Dad, I tried to snuggle a little closer to Mom. Then, in the pre-dawn light, I could see that Mom was packing her suitcase as quietly as possible. Instantly, I was wide awake!

"Mom!' I hollered. "Are you leaving?"

"It's not safe for me here, Steph," she explained, "but I think you're safe. I just found out something about your father that he didn't want me to know and confronted him on the issue."

"Oh, Mom!" I was so torn; do I stay with Dad, or go with Mom? Dad can be so nice—he lets me do whatever I want. Mom is strict, and I would be able to continue to attend home school if I went with her…I hate moving…but Mom would be alone…

Oh, God, what should I do? Help me know what to do. This decision will affect me for the rest of my life!

Suddenly, from the woods nearby, came the beautiful call of a bird singing the words, "Go-go-go…leave-leave-leave…go-go-go…leave-leave-leave." I distinctly heard the words being repeated among the trees outside the window! There was no mistaking the message! I quickly packed and left with my mother. And that has made all the difference. She is my spiritual guide, my confidante, and my very best friend.

---

*pseudonym

Note from the author: a large butcher knife was later uncovered in Stephanie's parent's bedroom and it was verified that her father had returned to the room that last night planning to inflict harm to one or possibly both of them.

*Beloved, think it not strange concerning
the fiery trial which is to try you,
as though some strange thing happened unto you:
but rejoice, inasmuch as ye are partakers of Christ's sufferings;
that, when His glory shall be revealed,
ye may be glad also with exceeding joy.*

—1 Peter 4:12, 13

Singing in the Dark

*In the full light of day,
and in hearing of the music of other voices,
the caged bird will not sing the song that his master
seeks to teach him.
He learns a snatch of this, a trill of that,
but never a separate and entire melody.
But the master covers the cage,
and places it where the
bird will listen to the one song he is to sing.
In the dark, he tries and tries again
to sing that song until it is learned,
and he breaks forth in perfect melody.
Then the bird is brought forth,
and ever after he can sing that song in the light.
Thus God deals with His children.
He has a song to teach us,
and when we have learned it amid
the shadows of affliction we can sing it ever afterward.*

—Ellen G. White

The Frail Bird's Song

As I walked into the garden
A little bird hopped by.
He cocked his little head just so
And looked toward the sky.

I looked a little closer as
I wondered, now, just why
Would he walk within the garden
When it seemed that he should fly?

His little wing was broken
And his feathers torn a bit.
He'd walk awhile, and turn around,
And, then, he'd seem to sit.

But, then, he opened wide his mouth
And sang a lovely song!
He seemed to sing of happiness
Like there was nothing wrong.

Yes, he was really happy
And that was plain to see.
His song rang out in thankfulness,
"I'm sure God cares for me!"

Oh, God, forgive me when I fret
And think that all is wrong.
May I lift my head in thankfulness
And sing the frail bird's song.

—Mary K. Donesky

Unnumbered Immensity

*He who upholds the unnumbered worlds throughout immensity,
at the same time cares for the wants of the little brown sparrow
that sings its humble song without fear.
When men go forth to their daily toil, as when they engage in prayer;
when they lie down at night, and when they rise in the morning;
when the rich man feasts in his palace,
or when the poor man gathers his children about the scanty board,
each is tenderly watched by the heavenly Father.
No tears are shed that God does not notice. ...
If we would but fully believe this, all undue anxieties would be dismissed. ...
We should then enjoy a rest of soul to which many have long been strangers. ...
In the varied gifts of God in nature we see but the faintest gleaming of His glory.*

—Ellen G. White

Skip to Me, Lou!

A friend loveth at all times...

Proverbs 14:14

During an extended stay in a northern B.C. hotel, the staff became our family. Learning of my love of birds, the manager of the restaurant told me about the time her pre-teen daughters gifted their father with a budgie and the friendship that followed. I quickly captured the story, and then shared it with her.

"Oh, Linda!" Kate cried when she read the story. "You captured it! You converted a difficult time in our lives into a good memory. These are happy tears!"

The Birthday Gift

"What should we get Dad for his birthday?" Mindy* asked her sister. "It's almost here."

"I think he could use some companionship," Connie* replied. "Remember how he enjoyed the budgies we used to have here at home before he moved out?"

"Hey, that's a good idea, Mindy! There's a beautiful display at K-Mart, and we still have a cage or two left, here, don't we?"

They pooled their money, grabbed a cage, went to K-Mart, and spent several exciting minutes deciding which color of budgie their father might like best. Little did they realize they were choosing a unique character that would affect their father's life for the next five years when they chose a saucy yellow-headed youngster with a pale blue-green cape draped over his back—a color that the girls associated with a refreshing mint flavored sweet. With the bird installed in the cage, they purchased some seed and grit, and headed home with their prize.

"Surprise!" cried the girls in unison as they handed over their gift. Paul* was truly surprised; he never would have thought to get a budgie for himself! It would have been too painful a reminder of what should have been happier times.

"Beautiful color," he nodded approvingly at his daughters, giving them a smile that made their effort worthwhile. "Does he have a name?"

"No, you get to do that!" they assured him as they hugged him. "Sorry we gotta go now, Dad. Have fun!"

Still smiling, Paul set the cage in a prominent position in the living room and sat down to get acquainted. It didn't take long for him to decide that the name of his sprightly new friend would be Lou, as in "Skip, skip, skip to my Lou."

Happy Days

Whenever Paul called, his children could hear the smile in their father's voice. Inevitably he would relate some new antic Lou had either learned or invented. "Smartest bird I've ever seen!" Paul would say. "An' 'e sings, too!"

After the first week, Paul allowed his new friend to share in every activity possible. If Paul was eating, he would put a treat on his tongue or in his ear, and Lou would carefully remove it, much to his master's delight. When Paul was watching a NASCAR race or a hockey game on television, Lou would sit on his shoulder and holler excitedly right along with his master. Whatever the activity, Lou sang about it. Listening to music was Lou's favorite activity—he would sing along with whatever tune happened to be playing.

Skip to Me, Lou!

Lou loved bathing, too. He would show up any time he heard water running in the bathroom, reminding his master that he was ready to get wet. Paul hung some ropes, hoops, and swings in the shower. He even installed a tiny bird bath and hung a mirror in front of it. Lou bathed daily—and he sang in the shower, too!

Lou was such an integral part of Paul's life that he only went to his cage for seeds and bathroom breaks. Interestingly, after the first few days of freedom, he never relieved himself in the house, only in his cage.

From the very beginning, there was no question in Lou's mind as to his choice of where to sleep. Given the chance, he would perch on Paul's headboard, muttering softly while his master prepared for bed. Characteristically, he would wait until Paul was under the covers, then hop down onto his pillow, and murmur a soft lullaby into Paul's ear.

The diminutive songster slept on his master's pillow and always sang his wake-up call long before Paul was ready to rise. He had become used to sleeping later and later in his ever-deepening discouragement. Lou became his caring, if demanding, nurse. In Lou's world, when the sun was up, it was time to sing yourself awake. It's difficult to ignore a budgie's breakfast song, especially if he's a good friend, a great singer, and leaning into your ear. Gradually, Paul was getting up a little earlier each day until he was, once again, looking on the brighter side of life.

With more daylight and Lou's unstoppable songs lifting his spirits, Paul's physical and emotional health improved. He felt so good that he set up the first Christmas tree he'd had since living on his own. When he was finished, he turned to the bird and said, "Go find a spot in the tree so I can take a nice picture of you!"

Lou chirped and flew to the tree, arranging himself artistically among the boughs. There was a click, a bright light, and a priceless Kodak® moment was captured. Commenting on the unique "ornament" that was nestled in his tree, Paul collected many compliments from the friends who received his Christmas card that year.

It didn't matter to Lou if there were days that his master did not feel like entertaining him. Little Lou was a faithful companion to the very end.

Such Sweet Songs

For five years he continued to perch on Paul's shoulder while he watched TV, on his kitchen chair when he ate, and on his pillow when he slept. The day Paul found little Lou at the bottom of his cage was as sad a day as he could remember. He had lost a wonderful friend: a comrade who'd been so patient with his grumbling that he didn't care to be disagreeable anymore, a buddy who was always there for him regardless of his mood, a confidante who had listened patiently and transformed his doubts into such splendid songs that he just could not stay depressed.

By then, Paul had quit smoking, but his lungs had taken a beating and failed at last. He went into hospice care not too long after Lou passed away. Before he breathed his last, Paul made sure to tell his daughters that their thoughtful gift had brought him more happiness than he could express.

"Best years of my life!" he assured his now teen-aged daughters. "Lou was a real friend! Thanks, again, for choosing him as my birthday gift!"

Everyone needs a friend like Lou—someone who is there when you need some company, who lifts your spirit when you are down, and who always…no matter what happens…has a song to share.

---
*People's names have been changed

To a Skylark

Hail to thee, blithe Spirit!
Bird thou never wert,
That from Heaven, or near it,
Pourest thy full heart
In profuse strains of unpremeditated art.

Higher still and higher
From the earth thou springest
Like a cloud of fire;
The blue deep thou wingest,
And singing still dost soar, and soaring ever singest.

In the golden lightning
Of the sunken sun
O'er which clouds are bright'ning,
Thou dost float and run,
Like an unbodied joy whose race is just begun.

The pale purple even
Melts around thy flight;
Like a star of Heaven
In the broad daylight
Thou art unseen, but yet I hear thy shrill delight:

Keen as are the arrows
Of that silver sphere,
Whose intense lamp narrows
In the white dawn clear
Until we hardly see—we feel that it is there.

All the earth and air
With thy voice is loud.
As, when night is bare,
From one lonely cloud
The moon rains out her beams, and heaven is overflowed.

What thou art we know not;
What is most like thee?
From rainbow clouds there flow not
Drops so bright to see
As from thy presence showers a rain of melody.

Like a poet hidden
In the light of thought,
Singing hymns unbidden,
Till the world is wrought
To sympathy with hopes and fears it heeded not:

Like a high-born maiden
In a palace tower,
Soothing her love-laden
Soul in secret hour
With music sweet as love, which overflows her bower:

Like a glow-worm golden
In a dell of dew,
Scattering unbeholden
Its aerial hue
Among the flowers and grass, which screen it from the view:

Like a rose embowered
In its own green leaves,
By warm winds deflowered,
Till the scent it gives
Makes faint with too much sweet these heavy-winged thieves.

Sound of vernal showers
On the twinkling grass,
Rain-awakened flowers,
All that ever was
Joyous, and clear, and fresh, thy music doth surpass.

Teach us, sprite or bird,
What sweet thoughts are thine:
I have never heard
Praise of love or wine
That panted forth a flood of rapture so divine.

Chorus hymeneal
Or triumphal chaunt
Matched with thine, would be all
But an empty vaunt—
A thing wherein we feel there is some hidden want.

What objects are the fountains
Of thy happy strain?
What fields, or waves, or mountains?
What shapes of sky or plain?
What love of thine own kind? What ignorance of pain?

With thy clear keen joyance
Languor cannot be:
Shadow of annoyance
Never came near thee:
Thou lovest, but ne'er knew love's sad satiety.

Waking or asleep,
Thou of death must deem
Things more true and deep
Than we mortals dream,
Or how could thy notes flow in such a crystal stream?

> We look before and after,
> And pine for what is not:
> Our sincerest laughter
> With some pain is fraught;
> Our sweetest songs are those that tell of saddest thought.
>
> Yet if we could scorn
> Hate, and pride, and fear;
> If we were things born
> Not to shed a tear,
> I know not how thy joy we ever should come near.
>
> Better than all measures
> Of delightful sound,
> Better than all treasures
> That in books are found,
> Thy skill to poet were, thou scorner of the ground!
>
> Teach me half the gladness
> That thy brain must know,
> Such harmonious madness
> From my lips would flow
> The world should listen then, as I am listening now!
>
> *—Percy B. Shelley*

Troubadour

As birds unto the genial homeland fly,
The winter's cold and lowering skies to flee,
So seeks my soul Thy gracious presence here,
And finds, O God, its rest and peace in Thee.

—David Levy

To love much is to hurt much…every once in a while. My good friend Michelle recently lost her father and she is hurting. But there is a beautiful buffer to her loss. Michelle's father, Rick Settle, suffered from Parkinson's disease. Her mother, Laverne, kept Rick at home right to the end, keeping him interested in daily living. About the same time that Laverne was running out of incentives, along came Troubadour. Was the rooster redeemed to fulfill a special assignment? I, for one, am convinced. See what you think of Michelle's account of welcomed wings.

    I had an idyllic childhood—a comfortable country home with parents who escorted their three daughters into adulthood with health of body, soundness of mind, and a firm spiritual foundation. We three girls learned early that spending time in the garden resulted in better food on the table. Dad sold Christian literature, so we learned to love stories and meaningful books. Mom taught us to sew, cook, and make good bread. Our family experienced a strong filial bond tromping through the great out-of-doors together that city children might miss; we hiked regularly in the woods, learned survival skills, old-fashioned remedies, and memorized Scripture and hymns that have sustained me through countless trials.

At the end of each day, we three girls would sit in a semi-circle at Daddy's feet while he strummed his guitar and sang hymns. My earliest memories are of learning to harmonize. I reminisce about my early years with a comfortable feeling of nostalgia, grateful for the strong bond that my parents and I have enjoyed.

The Bonding

Daddy made me feel so special. He and I both had a great love for birds and decided that we would get some chickens. Our colorful collection of hens and roosters became my exclusive bond with the man I most admired. We named our chickens; I recall Henny, Penny, and a rooster named Big Red, who regularly joined the cats for breakfast. Big Red became my special favorite, and his "wake-up" call became my beloved serenade.

Through the years, the song of the rooster increased in comfort; no matter what discouraging circumstance I faced—a rooster crowing brought with it a feeling of warmth and security. I was a country girl, forever, and so I managed to find country homes where we could enjoy the out-of-doors and have some animals, including at least one rooster.

Daddy taught me to love music. He was a great musician, able to master any instrument he set his hands on. I respected him for this talent (and am thankful that he passed this on to my children). One of my favorite songs was one he wrote himself to capture his own childhood.

Home Sweet Home

Everybody rushing everywhere, not much time to stop or care,
You sure can get a feelin' that you're all alone;
And sometimes I get to thinkin', sometimes I get to even wishin'—
Wishin' I could head back to my home.

Troubadour

Chorus:
I'd like to be where the living is easy, in a place called home sweet home,
Where the music is playing softly, in a place where I'm not alone;
Where the sweet melody of the bird comes drifting on the gentle breeze of dawn,
I'd like to be where the living is easy, in a place called home sweet home.

Pot of coffee in the making, in the oven biscuits baking,
On the griddle, hot cakes cooking, another day has just begun;
I remember those times together, Mama, Papa, me and my brother,
How I miss those days of home.

I can still smell that old home cooking, feel the warmth
from the wood stove burning,
Still hear my mama sweetly singing, though the years have come and gone;
I remember those times together, mama, papa, me and my brother
How I miss those days of home.

Every evening, we gathered around Daddy in the living room and sang favorite hymns together as he played his beautiful black guitar: *The Old Rugged Cross, Shall We Gather at the River, Abide With Me, I Come to the Garden Alone*, and *Rock of Ages*. Later, the words to these songs, imprinted indelibly in childhood, buoyed me up during a few very stormy years and guided me gently back to the fold.

For as long as I can remember, Daddy wrote poems and songs. I recall going to sleep listening to him perfecting the meter and tune of some new creation. Through our teen years, his concern for his three daughters' choices deepened. He would sometimes plead with us to carefully consider the path we chose and reiterate the importance of staying close to Jesus. He captured his advice in a poem that he recited to me, with tears in his eyes, when I left home.

Jesus Wasn't There

The world with all its glittering ways was looking mighty fine,
So I thought and contemplated and decided it was time
To take a break, and have a fling, and do that which was rare,
So I went out to the cinema, but—Jesus wasn't there.

It wasn't really all that bad; I then thought sometime later—
Oh, a little bit of violence, but its pleasure proved the greater.
And even then, I knew deep down, my Lord would not have gone,
I subtly reasoned with myself that I had done no wrong.

The days went by, the weeks, the months, an occasion did arise
When the world, with some more glitter, looked appealing to my eyes.
A music festival of rock was coming to our town.
I'd kinda learned to like the beat, and could not turn it down.

The concert lasted several days, and then I left in haste;
Some of the things that happened there made me feel out of place.
But I had really liked the sounds, they made my feelings flare,
Yet a small voice whispered softly that—Jesus wasn't there.

The years were passing swiftly now, and many things I'd done
When my eyes beheld a pleasure that was sure to help my fun.
I shall not tell the path I chose, the people in despair,
Only know, I walked alone, for—Jesus wasn't there.

That small voice that I used to hear was very silent now,
But I really didn't seem to miss its pleadings anyhow.
The world, it kept me occupied, I had no time to spare,
And it really didn't matter if that small voice wasn't there.

I continued down this path I chose, feeling satisfied,
When suddenly the world was filled with strife on every side;
People breaking out in boils, turning raw and sore;
A scorching sun, and hailstones weighing sixty pounds or more!

*"It's time to change my ways," said I, "yes, change my ways, in fact,
I'd better read my Bible more, and straighten up my act."
So, I read a bit of Luke and John, and then knelt down in prayer,
And I prayed, and prayed, and prayed, and prayed,
but—Jesus wasn't there.*

Passing the Baton

In spite of my poor choices, the Lord blessed me with three wonderful children who are my pride and joy. When a fire destroyed all our earthly goods, we managed to escape our abusive situation. The years that followed were some of the lowest, and highest points of my life. Money was always tight and sometimes even the next meal was an unknown factor, but we never went hungry, and the music lifted our spirits created glimpses of a better land for those who loved their Savior.

Uplifting influences came to us in strange and wondrous ways, sometimes in direct answer to prayer. Books were a source of endless pleasure. My children were avid readers, especially loving allegories about pathways to heaven such as *Pilgrim's Progress*, *Hind's Feet on High Places*, and *Mountains of Spices*. They also loved gardening and learned eating healthfully. Their greatest love, however, was making music. Instruments came to us in interesting ways; we discovered a nice accordion in a thrift store. A clarinet, harmonicas in many keys, three guitars, and even a keyboard were given to us. Daddy gave my oldest son a beautiful guitar. Each child had a music bond with their grandfather. There was nothing they enjoyed more than a visit with Grandpa, returning to him his own heritage of song. And Daddy loved it!

The children traded instruments with each other so that they could master each new "toy." Eventually, each of them specialized in one or two instruments, but could play a little on each one. They committed many hymns to memory and were often called upon to perform special music at church.

Dark Clouds

Today, whatever problem comes our way, from illness to discouragement, we choose to face it sitting in our sacred circle, lifting each other's spirit through music, even though we sometimes sit in complete darkness, both physically and emotionally. Recognizing the intrusions of Giant Despair, one of us will grab a violin, mandolin, guitar, banjo, banjitar, or harmonica, and begin playing or singing away our troubles. Eventually we all join in. Heavenly joys became more real to us than the troubles that press us down. I can thank my father for that way of escape from trouble.

When my father was diagnosed with Parkinson's disease, he finally gave up his chickens, but he kept playing and singing until he could no longer lift his guitar. Even then, he wrote new songs. One such poem became my personal favorite.

A Certain Kind of Person

It takes a certain kind of person, to love his fellow man.
It takes a certain kind of person to help others when he can.
It takes a certain kind of person, to greet you with a smile.
It takes a certain kind of person, to be cheerful all the while.

So though your troubles seem too many,
Good fortunes seem too few,
Remember, there is always someone
Less fortunate than you.

Don't think about the days gone by
Or wrongs that have been done
Don't fret about tomorrow,
For tomorrow never comes.

Troubadour

Do your best for today
And as the days go on,
You'll find that there's much more in life
For you and everyone.

When I was twenty-six, three years after Daddy was diagnosed with Parkinson's disease, I decided to learn to play the guitar. In spite of the distance between our homes, we enjoyed many musical weekends together. It was a joy to watch my father teach my children some of what he had learned. As with me, Daddy was always there for me to help my children discern life's lessons, and loved them unconditionally, too.

Rooster on a Mission

Mom took care of Dad at home, even when it was more than she should have attempted. As Dad's disease progressed, he was tempted to stay indoors more, but the God of the great outdoors sent him a very personal invitation to come out and enjoy the sunshine.

Their good neighbor, Ola, learned about an Old English Game rooster with shining black tail feathers, golden neck, and big red comb (a show bird such as artists paint and sculpt), that was destined to become chicken soup. She intervened and was awarded the Troubadour who greeted her every morning with his sun-up song. The rescued bird had been at Ola's house for only a few days when the lustrous cock went visiting. It appeared he had an assignment.

One sunny morning, while Dad was asleep in his easy chair after breakfast, Mom heard an incessant tapping at her kitchen door. When she answered the summons, she was surprised to discover a beautiful rooster looking up at her—his bright red comb, golden cape, and long black tail feathers hoarding the richness of the early morning sun. This troubadour of reveille stood on tiptoe, peeking in at Daddy, as if asking him to come out and play.

"Honey, come and look at this, would you!" Mom called to Daddy. "You have a visitor! The most beautiful rooster I have ever seen!" In spite of his exhaustion, Daddy couldn't resist an invitation to meet their caller. The Troubadour came daily after that first morning. Daddy took to keeping cookie crumbs in his pockets for his new friend.

It warmed Mom's heart to watch Daddy and Troubadour tackle a job together. Whether Daddy was trying to fix a bike or tending the garden, that magnificent rooster was right beside him, poking his beautiful golden head into gears or geraniums, crooning contentedly. When, eventually, Daddy ran out of strength, he would shuffle over to the car and sit down in the back seat. Troubadour would stand quietly beside him, while Daddy gently stroked the rooster—the trembling of his hand reduced to a gentle massage slowly vibrating through Troubadour's silky feathers.

Unwelcome Message

The phone call that I never wanted to hear came on October 20, 2015. Mom's tearful voice informed me that paramedics were trying to revive Daddy where he had collapsed onto the table while eating breakfast. When they had a pulse, he was rushed to the hospital. It was time to make the thirteen-hour drive to embrace Daddy one last time, to tell him that I loved him.

We dropped everything, quickly packed our bags, borrowed a car, said a prayer for safety and drove through the night to the home of my childhood. I immediately phoned the hospital.

"If you want to see your father before he passes," said the nurse who answered, "come now."

As I walked into the hospital room, I wanted so much for it to be just a bad dream. Tears flowed freely as I looked down upon Daddy's shrunken frame, a mere shadow of the strong hero of my childhood. I held onto his big hands and told him I loved him, that one day soon Jesus would return and call him from the grave, and that we would meet again.

Daddy was hooked up to IV lines, monitoring wires, and a breathing machine. When it was established that he was unresponsive, it was decided to remove his breathing tube. He was not expected to respond to his surroundings, or even to keep breathing, but for the next three days we took turns holding his hand, talking to him, and trying to imagine life without him. Once, when I leaned close, he looked into my eyes.

"I love you Daddy," I said past the lump in my throat just about the size of the eggs we used to gather, side-by-side, each morning. He seemed to focus. A tear fell from his eye. Though the medical team would not affirm the possibility, I believe Daddy told me goodbye.

On October 30, 2015, at the viewing the night before his funeral, I sat on the floor beside his casket, and recorded the thoughts that flooded my mind. I read it at his funeral the next day.

As I take a last look at my precious Dad, he's laying very peacefully in this grey coffin. Death has taken control, but Jesus has said, "Death has no sting." He will, and has, overcome the devil. Daddy, I look at you and remember the precious memories, the special moments, your teasing, your caring; the times we spent as a family and your melodious voice; your guitar playing; the times we travelled as a family. Daddy, I love you. I wish I could go back and hold onto those moments more securely. I know without a doubt I will see you again! But while on this earth, I will miss you dearly, my heart is broken, but you always have a spot in my heart. Thank you Daddy, for all the love you gave me.
Love you,
Michelle

Memorial Park

That evening, after the funeral and graveside service, I told my sister that I was going to go to Daddy's grave. When she asked why, I told her that I needed to see how his grave site would look after he was buried so that I could visit the site in my memory.

I dressed warmly to deflect the November chill, not knowing exactly what to expect when I arrived. I had to see Daddy's final resting place devoid of the crowd, the activity, and distractions of the day. I wasn't sure what I was going to feel about his final resting place—I only knew that I desperately needed a peaceful moment to store in my memory.

Even without the multitude of flower arrangements, wreaths and flowering plants placed artistically over the grave, I was awestruck. Daddy's resting place was exactly as it should be—majestic trees, surrounded by acres of beautiful green grass. I knelt among the flowers and said my private goodbye. It was finished. It was beautiful.

Evening Serenade

As I was kneeling there, two hens and a picturesque rooster with long black tail feathers, a golden cape, and bright red comb strutted past. The rooster glanced at the darkening sky and addressed the setting sun with his evening serenade. No song on earth could have meant more to me in that moment than to hear a rooster crow, a rooster that, in actual fact, looked exactly like Daddy's precious Troubadour!

Hearing that evening serenade over my father's grave site was a solemn benediction. My heart was comforted. The timely reminder of our bond seemed to give me permission to begin my healing journey. My Daddy was resting peacefully, just as he would have wanted, with a beautiful rooster tracking sunrise and sunset with his favorite song.

Sometimes the pain of losing Daddy is more than I feel I can bear—as if part of my own heart died with him. Some days it is difficult to grasp the fact that he is gone. Until I see him again, I will sing the old hymns about the love of Jesus and take care of his beautiful black guitar—the one that Mom sent with me as we headed home after Daddy's funeral. I look forward to one day lifting the old MANN from its shiny leather case, and to the best of my ability, reverently play a song in loving memory of the man who gave me life, and the precious Man who died for me to make possible the day I will see my Daddy again.

I'll see you in the morning Daddy. If the splendor of heaven momentarily blinds us, we can just hold hands, close our eyes, and wait, as you said so long ago, "…the sweet melody of the bird comes drifting on the gentle breeze of dawn."

Genius

A skylark in a bygone day
Mounted the sky
Singing its long familiar lay,
And passing by
Went men and women up and down
With hearts unstirred.
Theirs was the business of the town—
But Shelley heard.

The air had long borne those liquid notes
For ages long;
From countless million golden throats
Had poured that song,
And still the people sold and bought
And toiled for fame.
'Tis but a bird that sings, they thought
Till Shelley came.

Enraptured by that lovely thing
And touched with pain,
With every nerve set quivering
Like leaves in rain,
He stood the while the twilight rang
With chords divine,
And caught the song the skylark sang
In deathless line.

Who knows what beauty and what grace
Are hidden still,
Buried among the commonplace
Of mart and mill,
Waiting with patience through the years,
As did the lark,
Until the genius appears
Their charms to mark?

—*Edgar A. Guest*

Prisoners of Hope

I was in prison, and ye came unto me.

—Matthew 25:36

Is there a more hopeless situation than prison, an internment camp, death row? Two of the three individuals described in the following stories endured unthinkable tortures at the hands of their captors. With permission, I bring you three accounts of birds who delivered hope in times of utter desperation.

The Birdman of Alcatraz

Robert Stroud was probably the most famous inmate ever to reside on Alcatraz. Convicted of murder in 1909, he was sent to serve out his sentence at McNeil Island, a Federal penitentiary in Washington State. After repeated assaults on personnel and fellow inmates, he was transferred to Leavenworth Federal Penitentiary in Kansas. In 1916, after Stroud was refused a visit with his brother, he killed a prison guard. Sentenced to death by hanging, and he was ordered to await his death sentence in solitary confinement. In 1920, after his mother desperately pleaded for his life, President Woodrow Wilson commuted his death sentence to life imprisonment without parole. As a result of Stroud's unpredictable and violent outbursts, Stroud lived out his sentence in solitary confinement.

After finding an injured bird in the recreation yard at Leavenworth, Stroud developed a keen interest in canaries. He was initially allowed to breed the birds and maintain a lab inside two adjoining cells. It was felt that this activity would provide for productive use of his time. During his years in Leavenworth he raised nearly 300 canaries, carefully studying their habits and physiology, making medicines for their ailments, and authoring two books on canaries and their diseases. His book, *Stroud's Digest on the Diseases of Birds*, published in 1943, was an important work in the field of canary research. After learning that some of the lab equipment that he had requested for canary research was being used to distill alcohol, it was decided to transfer Stroud to Alcatraz. For the next seventeen years, he was allowed to continue his research but denied further publication rights. In 1959, with failing health, he was transferred to the Medical Center for Federal Prisoners in Springfield, Missouri. On November 21, 1963, he was found dead by his close friend and fellow inmate, Morton Sobell, a spy who revealed atomic secrets to the Russians.

How can a heart, with such a violent nature as Robert Stroud's, be reached by a wounded bird? The heart of the Birdman of Alcatraz, a killer that no one could reach, was softened by the songs of canaries.

Corrie ten Boom

It is likely that everyone in the world knows the name Corrie ten Boom— her lowly birth into a Dutch watchmaker's family, her father's work in aiding the Jews during WWII, and the capture and subsequent death of her family in concentration camps. Corrie herself, though tortured and reduced to a mere skeleton in the camps, held as fast to her faith in God as did her family members. She was eventually released, by a miracle, to tell her story to the world. One incident that was a tremendous encouragement to her, in the face of extreme mistreatment, was the day the skylark visited the death camp during roll call.

"Morning roll call at *Ravensbruck* was often the hardest time of the day. By 4:30 a.m. we had to be standing outside our barracks in the black predawn chill, in blocks of one hundred women, ten wide, ten deep.

"Names were never used in the concentration camp. It was part of the plan to dehumanize the prisoners—to take away their dignity of life and their worth before God and man. I was known simply as Prisoner 66730.

"Roll call sometimes lasted three hours. Every day the sun rose a little later and the icy-cold wind blew a little stronger. Standing in the gray of the dawn, I would try to repeat, through shivering lips, that verse of Scripture which had come to mean so much to me: 'Who shall separate us from the love of Christ? shall tribulation, or distress, or persecution, or famine, or nakedness, or peril, or sword? As it is written, for thy sake we are killed all the day long; we are accounted as sheep for the slaughter' (Rom. 8:35–36). In all this there was an overwhelming victory through Jesus who had proved His love for me by dying on the cross.

"But there came a time when repeating the words did not help. I needed more. 'Oh God,' I prayed, 'reveal Yourself somehow.'

"Then one morning the woman directly in front of me sank to the ground. In a moment a young woman guard was standing over her, a whip in her hand.

"'Get up,' she screamed in a rage. 'How dare you think you can lie down when everyone else is standing!'

"I could hardly bear to see what was happening in front of me. *Surely this is the end of us all*, I thought. Then suddenly a skylark started to sing high in the sky. The sweet, pure notes of the bird rose on the still cold air. Every head turned upward, away from the carnage before us, listening to the song of the skylark soaring over the crematorium. The words of the psalmist ran through my mind: 'For as the heaven is high above the earth, so great is [God's] mercy toward them that fear Him' (Ps. 103:11)."

(*Tramp for the Lord* by Corrie ten Boom, ©1974 by Corrie ten Boom and Jamie Buckingham. Used by permission of CLC Publications. May not be further reproduced. All rights reserved.)

Bruce's Song in the Night

Bruce Olson had worked among the Motilone Indians for twenty-eight years creating schools, churches, teaching health principles, offering malaria medicines, and gaining the respect of the tribesmen before he was captured by the communist-inspired National Liberation Army (NLA, or ELN—Ejérercito de Liberación Nacional) at the border of Columbia and Venezuela. He was intermittently tortured for several months by this group at twelve different prisons, spending most nights with his arms tied behind his back. He had been captured during the rainy season so his clothes were always wet.

When he was finally allowed to have a Bible, some of the soldiers began asking questions about salvation. At the last prison camp, Bruce became very ill with diverticulitis and hemorrhaged internally. The pain was intense. As he lay helpless, trying to cope with the pain, the song of a bird seemed to encase him. Could it be a mirla bird? Mirlas do not sing at night. He wondered if he was delirious as variations of the beautiful song repeated itself in minor tonal chants while he passed in and out of consciousness. The song carried a familiar ring, as if he had heard it before, but for several hours he could not place the melody. Then, in a moment of clarity he understood—the mirla was mimicking a Motilone rendition of a song that Bruce had taught them about the resurrection of Jesus. The notes, and message of that song, carried him through the painful night.

In the morning he heard the guerrillas discussing the strange song that they had heard repeated through the night. One of the soldiers said he thought that it may have been an angel singing to the prisoner that was to be executed, not just a bird. As the soldiers made ready for his execution, Bruce wondered, too. Here is the actual account of the execution from the prologue to *Bruchko*, written by Robert Walker.

> Three days earlier, Bruce had been given the ultimatum (after many days of painful indoctrination by the communist-inspired NLA): either join them or be executed... .
>
> Over the past twenty-eight years, on a number of occasions his faith had been tested almost to the point of death. In those times the Lord had sustained his confidence in Him. Bruce had come to the jungles of Colombia because

Such Sweet Songs

He wanted him there. So long as he remained obedient to that vision he had to believe that the Lord would provide for whatever his needs would be.

But he'd never faced execution before. As Bruce could see the commander handing rifles to the men who were to be his executioners, curiously the memory of the ineffable message of the mirla came back to him.

Had this been why the Lord had given him the mirla bird on that fateful night? It certainly seemed possible. After all, Jesus said He would never leave or forsake him. There was no way he could not believe Him now.

Bruce could only smile sadly as he looked at the guerrillas in their shabby uniforms. Many had been present at his discussion on the Bible. More than half of these guerrillas had made some sort of profession for Jesus Christ as their Savior. Bruce felt sorry for them. Had they refused the order to participate in this execution they themselves would be shot.

Cartridges were handed out, and he could hear the click as they were slid into the chambers of their guns. At the commander's orders, the guerrillas slowly raised their rifles. Then came the command: "Fire!"

Bruce waited for the thud of slugs in his body. None came. The shots were blanks.

(Bruce Olson, *Bruchko*, Charisma House, Lake Mary, FL, copyright 2006, used by permission)

Upon his release, the commander gave Bruce no explanation for his actions except that it was a "mistake" that he was captured.

Hope

Hope is the thing with feathers
That perches in the soul,
And sings the tune—without the words,
And never stops at all.

And sweetest in the gale is heard;
And sore must be the storm
That could abash the little bird
That kept so many warm.

I've heard it in the chillest land,
And on the strangest sea;
Yet, never, in extremity,
It asked a crumb of me.

—Emily Dickinson

Possession

The woods and fields and trees are ours
With all their lavish wealth of flowers;
The stars at night which brightly shine,
The morning sun, are yours and mine;
   And added to such joys as these
   We stand possessors of the breeze.

Who calls us poor, because we lack
The nation's printed yellow-back,
   Is only partly right. We share
   God's mercy with the millionaire.
   No more of beauty can he see
Than that which smiles at you and me.

We won the earth for all our time.
Wherever summer roses climb
For us to gaze on, they are ours,
Where're a snow-capped mountain towers
   We've but to turn our heads to say
   That splendid thing is ours to-day.

To us the blue of heaven belongs.
Ours are the wild birds' merry songs.
   Silver and gold are scarce, but oh,
What countless charms the days bestow!
   And here, right at our humble doors,
   Of splendor we have endless stores.

      —*Edgar A. Guest*

The Weaver

He healeth the broken in heart, and bindeth up their wounds.

—Psalm 147:3

A test comes to each of us when we experience pain, discomfort, anxiety: what will we choose to turn to for comfort and reassurance? We may be tempted to reach for our own convenient devices, such as food or drugs, or fall into the pit of anger, bitterness and depression. We can try to cope by anesthetizing our pain or diverting our attention from the issue…or, we can choose to work through the discomfort by feeling it, taking our pain to The Comforter, and allowing ourselves to be enfolded in the Father's arms and reassured of His tender, and compassionate love.

Far from home, bereaved, broken-hearted and alone, Tamara could neither sleep, nor face the demanding duties of the long day ahead. She was overwhelmed and at a loss to relieve her emotional pain. Thankfully, she had "ears to hear" and "eyes to see" the message of love, sent from above, that enabled her to function so she could continue to help those who depended upon her.

In September of 2014, long term missionaries to Tanzania, Africa—Doug and Tamara Schoch and their son Joshua—were called to be in two places at once. Since Doug was in the midst of a lengthy evangelistic series near their home in Mafinga, Tamara and Joshua agreed to drive the seven hours to Haneti to help out. Their days were busy with medical outreach; each evening they'd present a health lesson just before the evangelistic meetings. Tamara conducted the lessons in English while Joshua translated into Swahili.

On the first Saturday after Tamara and Joshua arrived, they spoke at a local church. During a break in services, Tamara and Joshua slipped outside the building and noticed several young village children playing roughly with a puppy. The children, one by one, would put a foot under the belly of the little puppy, between her front and back feet, and flip her quickly onto her back where she would land with a thud in the dirt. They found great amusement in watching her scramble to right herself over and over. Having a soft heart and great love for animals, Tamara couldn't stand by to watch this mistreatment of one of God's little creatures.

"Stop! Leave her alone." Tamara commanded in the local language. The small mob of children quickly backed away when they saw the "missionary woman" coming toward them with a stern look. The puppy was timid and sweet. As Tamara and Joshua petted, played with, and protected the little dog, they also befriended the group of children who had gradually begun gathering 'round again. They continued to be gentle and kind to the puppy as they spoke with the watching children, encouraging them to treat animals well. The little brown and white puppy enjoyed this kindness, and was soon trying to follow them back into the church.

Pleased with the white missionary's interest in the puppy and the children, one of the adults who witnessed some of this interaction asked if Tamara would like to have the puppy. To the locals, the pup was just another mouth to feed. It was difficult for a poor family to come up with enough food for themselves, let alone a puppy.

"I do enjoy playing with the puppy," Tamara assured the person. "Give me some time to think about it and to speak with my family." Joshua was enthusiastic about keeping the pup, as he had wanted a dog for a very long time, and Doug's response was immediate.

The Weaver

"Sure! Bring the puppy home with you!"

The little puppy belonged to the herds-boy who had been watching his family's cows near the church. A church member made the arrangements with the owners of the little dog. When the evangelistic meetings in Haneti were finished, Tamara and Joshua brought the energetic new puppy home.

Before coming to Africa, the Schoch family had listened to *Jungle Doctor*, a series of audio books about a physician who had worked with the Gogo tribe in Tanzania. Words and phrases of the tribal language were spoken in the audio series, and they had learned that one word, *chibwa*, meant *little dog*. Since the village of Haneti is in Gogo territory, and their little dog was from this tribe's land, the family decided to name their new little bundle of enthusiasm Chibwa.

The happy pup blended right into the Schoch household, responding to their loving care with many a joyful wag of her little tail. Although Chibwa belonged to the whole family, Doug immediately recognized that the pup was really Tamara's dog … as if little Chibwa understood that it was to Tamara that she owed her good fortune.

Chibwa was a very smart dog, and quickly learned to obey. During her first year she became very ill with a local, deadly disease called "Mufindi," thought by locals to be contracted when an animal consumes certain insects (usually grasshoppers that have been feasting on a toxic plant). When ingested the toxin affects the nervous system, first causing victims to become easily frightened, then progressing to slight foaming at the mouth accompanied by loss of balance. The onset of the third stage brings frantic running, barking, and hiding in dark places, then finally severe convulsions … usually followed by death.

Immediately, Tamara emailed family and friends, including her good friend Heidi, requesting prayers for both Chibwa's recovery, and for wisdom to know how to help. Many prayers from around the world went up to the Heavenly Father, pleading for Chibwa's life to be spared. Not knowing what else to do, Tamara gave the little dog charcoal and watched over her constantly. She learned of a local herb that could be mixed with a little cooked egg that Chibwa ate in addition to regular doses of charcoal. With constant care and much prayer for more than a week, Tamara nursed the little dog back to health. Miraculously, Chibwa fully recovered! The family gave God all the credit for her healing ... surely He does care for all of His little creatures!

All that Chibwa knew how to do was love, and she did that very well. She licked faces and hands, and her short little tail wiggle-waggled her whole body.

Tamara received notice that she was needed to help with a series of seventeen evangelism meetings in the Mbeya region, five hours away from their home in Mafinga. Since Joshua was helping his father burn fire-breaks to protect the mission compound, Tamara faced the upcoming mission alone. It was a tearful farewell. She had been working in Mbeya less than a week when she received a disturbing message from Doug.

"Sad news." He texted. "Call me."

When Tamara was able to call, she learned that little Chibwa had been killed by a neighbor, a Christian man who lived on their mission compound. The agriculture school leaders had reported that a rabid dog was loose on the mission station. With Doug and Joshua being gone all day on fire duty, Chibwa must have been lonely. She managed to get out of the fence surrounding their home, through some loose boards, and went visiting. Unfortunately, the warning of a rabid dog had gone before her and alerted the neighbors to possible danger. When Chibwa entered the area where the Schoch's neighbor was working, he was frightened. He picked up a board and ended their beloved pet's life.

Tamara was crushed when she received the message. Though she tried to be brave until the end of the day, she found it impossible to stifle her tears. At the end of the day, behind the closed door of her hotel room, she broke down completely. Being unable to share her sorrow with Doug and Joshua made the tragedy more difficult to bear. Sometime after midnight she fell into a troubled sleep with the words of the man who killed her precious pet still ringing in her ears, "I am very sorry but it is not my fault."

The Weaver

Despite her lack of sleep, Tamara arose much earlier than usual. She found some comfort in her Bible reading, but she still felt unable to face the group of people who were helping with the evangelistic effort. She must be cheerful for the sake of those among whom she was working; but how could she invent a joy she did not feel? Wrestling with her sorrow, Tamara stayed in her room much later than usual. It was there, in her sanctuary of mourning, that a special chorus lifted her discouraged spirit to unexpected heights.

Tamara was weeping into her hands when she thought she heard tapping at her window. She peeked hesitatingly through the curtains but saw nothing. Then she heard the tapping again. Yes, someone *was* tapping on the window pane! Then she heard a chattering noise. Wiping her eyes, again she opened the curtain. Staring back at her was a weaver bird.

A beautiful African Masked Weaver (Ploceus velatus), his red eyes shining brightly, was optimistically inviting Tamara to face the day. Having left his own family, in order to deliver a very special message to a stranger, he continued to peck and chatter even with the curtain open, demanding Tamara's full attention. Finally assured of it, he flew to a well-lit nearby branch, allowing Tamara to appreciate the yellow and black patterns of his brilliant feathers. He nearly glittered in the bright sunlight.

Then, seeming to enjoy her attention and the opportunity to share his source of joy, the weaver flew to another tree whose branches were filled with a huge flock of beautiful finches and several other varieties of singing birds. Had they all been right outside Tamara's window every morning? She had neither seen nor heard a one! She opened her window to a symphony such as she had never heard before. After listening to the healing strains until her heart was comforted, Tamara flew to her laptop to email this experience to her long-time friend, Heidi, concluding her letter with these words:

God KNOWS I love to see and hear the birds. With the sun coming up and the beauty in the birds and plants, I know He is with me and will help me through each challenge. I hear the birds continuing their songs outside my window as I type this. Oh, how He wants me to know His love! I will make it through this day with my eyes on Him,

Upon receiving this message, Heidi remembered that Linda Franklin was collecting bird stories for a new volume of encouragement, and felt impressed to forward (with Tamara's permission) a sketch of this story. Tamara reiterated that she firmly believes that God was lovingly instructing her through this experience, and that, if that little weaver bird can face his day so cheerfully with his red eyes, surely she could too!

Tamara reports that they finished the efforts with about 400 baptisms at the 17 sites. She believes that her assistance in the evangelistic effort would not have been as effective without the encouragement of that joyful heavenly choir.

Angels Camp Fire

The angel of the LORD encampeth round about them that fear him, and delivereth them.

—Psalm 34:7

Mark Twain based his short story "The Celebrated Jumping Frog of Calaveras County" on a story he claimed he heard at the "Angels Hotel" in 1865. The event is commemorated with a Jumping Frog Jubilee each May at the Calaveras County Fairgrounds, just east of Angels Camp, California. Because of this, Angels Camp is sometimes referred to as "Frogtown."

The frog competition, however, was of little concern to the Howard family, who moved to Aunt Lucy's farm in the rolling hills above the town in 1943. "Do angels really camp here?" four-year-old Ellis wondered. Just before he reached his thirteenth birthday, he would receive his answer in a most unusual way.

The Howard family had always wanted a home in the country, but couldn't afford it. Then, wonder of wonders, old Aunt Lucy asked them to come and live with her in the hills about five miles from the little town of Angels Camp. She wasn't related to the Howards, but whatever family she did have never came to visit her or help with the farm. True, she was a little persnickety, but at 91, Ellis and his older brother David allowed that she was entitled to her opinions and learned to love her as the grandmother they didn't have.

Home in the Country

The boys enjoyed sharing in the farm chores among Aunt Lucy's colorful and friendly collection of animals: miniature ponies, pet skunks, dogs, chickens, peacocks, calves, angora rabbits, and angora goats. Ever afterward, the boys would consider Angels Camp as home. It was where they explored and discovered how things worked, it was where they became teen-agers, it was the place they "left home" from, and there were at least two miracles in which they felt the hand of angels. How they came to inherit the farm was the second miracle. It was the first miracle that would invoke a more potent feeling of gratefulness than the second. It was the first miracle that convinced them of the angels *encamped round about them to deliver them.*

    Money was tight. The boys' father, Clifford, was a paramedic (before it was classified as a vocation) and drove an ambulance for the town of Angels Camp. Their mother, Ada, worked nights at a tuberculosis hospital in Murphys, a few miles to the east. This left one parent, or Aunt Lucy, always at home with the boys, though they claimed they didn't need any supervision for their explorations on Aunt Lucy's 160 acres of wooded pastureland.

Angels on Patrol

The "Grade Road Pony Farm," as Aunt Lucy's place was called, most often boasted more than twenty Shetland ponies who earned their keep during the summer by giving rides to children. During local town celebrations, the Howards would sometimes set up a riding ring for the day. Children would stand in line with their dime impatiently waiting their turn to ride around the ring. Dave and Ellis kept the ponies groomed, and the tack shined and repaired. During the summer, they enjoyed saddling up and riding together when their chores were finished, which included patrolling the ditch.

It was dry country, but Aunt Lucy's pride and joy was her garden. She boasted delicacies that many folks in the valley couldn't seem to nurture to maturity. The ditch, an irrigation canal created by the previous owners, meandered across the hillside delivering an abundance of water to the house, barn, and garden. When her sons discovered a newborn foal in the ditch, Ada suddenly viewed the ditch as a threat.

"I don't want you boys going anywhere near that ditch!"

Not many days later, the household awakened to empty faucets. Ellis and David, responsible for keeping the ditch free of breaks, washouts, and leakage caused by gopher holes and cave-ins, had not been able to perform their usual maintenance to keep the water flowing. Forced to rethink her position, Ada realized that her ban may be interfering with more than just water. She began to appreciate how much the boys were learning about practical living on the farm. They were especially enthusiastic about Aunt Lucy's garden, helping her with watering, weeding, harvesting, and preserving food.

"Someone named the town Angels Camp for good reason," Ada thought as she lifted the ban and leaned a little heavier on prayer for her family's safety.

The Angel's Song

One day Aunt Lucy began feeling ill. It was eventually decided that she should go to the San Andreas County Hospital. While she was recuperating from her illness there, she fell and broke her hip. The Howards came to visit her two or three times a week during her recuperation. A nephew of hers visited once, but he was not friendly to the Howard family, and convinced Aunt Lucy to evict them. What happened next required a monumental interception to prevent the death of Clifford and his sons.

It was late when Clifford finished packing the first load of furniture into his truck in preparation for their move. He climbed the stairs to sleep in the boys' attic room that night since the downstairs bed was packed for next day's delivery to the house they had rented about ten miles away.

It was a warm night. The window was open. Through that window, sometime after midnight, Clifford heard a guardian angel sing; it wasn't quite the quality of tone one would normally associate with an angel's song, nevertheless, it served to rouse Cliff from a sound sleep.

"Help! Help! Help!" the sound was repeated from the top of the old oak tree beneath the boys' window.

Clifford sat straight up in bed. Why would that peacock be hollering in the middle of the night?

The peacocks were always quiet after they went to roost for the night, so Clifford roused enough to look out the window to see if he could establish the cause of the bird's alarm call. It was a beautiful, still night. None of the animals were stirring. As he considered the beauties of the peaceful countryside, the peacock called again.

"Help! Help! Help!" That was when Clifford smelled the smoke. He roused the boys, and together they quickly made their way downstairs. The stairwell was hot and hazy. The handrail and the wall were too hot to touch. The boys, with their father herding them out ahead of him, burst through the front door with seconds to spare before the entire house went up in flames.

Unfortunately, there was no one near enough to help. Or was there someone? Yes, Clifford caught sight of a man with a flashlight running down the hill. Clifford stumbled down the hill behind him, in the direction of the light.

"Help!" Clifford repeated the peacock's plea as he ran. The light went out. The peacock repeated Clifford's call for help. The man jumped into an older model pick-up and sped away down the hill. Too late for help, now, anyway. Clifford went back up the hill and stood beside his sons to watch the house, with most of the Howard's belongings and all of Aunt

Lucy's possessions, light up the night. Mesmerized by the inferno, they could hardly begin to fathom their loss.

Reclamation

It was eventually established that the fire was caused by arson. With Clifford's testimony of seeing the man with the flashlight running from the scene, the police questioned Lucy's nephew who lived only half a mile from Aunt Lucy's farm. He denied having anything to do with the fire, but he did say, "I didn't know there was anyone in the house! I thought Aunt Lucy asked them to leave a couple of weeks ago!"

The Howards continued to visit Aunt Lucy as she convalesced at the hospital in San Andreas. One day, Aunt Lucy made a proposal to Clifford. "Mr. Howard, if you'll rebuild a new house on the old foundation I'll provide the materials. I want you all to return to the farm."

Such Sweet Songs

Clifford and the boys cleaned up the burn site, temporarily roofed the basement of the old house with a tarp, and then installed a wood stove on which to cook their food. For a few months, the family slept in the barn with the animals, always with an affectionate glance at the guardian angel in the oak tree before snuggling into their sleeping bags.

The next year, Clifford's sons, now in their teens, helped their father finish building the house. The new house was larger, modernized. In spite of their losses, it seemed to the Howard family that everything had worked out for the best, kind of like the promise in the Good Book that they hadn't really understood so well before, about all things working together for good.

Aunt Lucy thought so, too. She loved her airy new bedroom with the big picture window that overlooked her beautiful valley. Before her death, she signed her farm over to the Howard family, who never forgot the night their guardian angel hollered loud enough to save their lives.

The peacock's is still Ellis' favorite bird song. He told me so himself, more than fifty years after his awakening.

What the Robin Told

The wind told the grasses,
And the grasses told the trees.

The trees told the bushes,
And the bushes told the bees.

The bees told the robin,
And the robin sang out clear:

Wake up! Wake up!
Spring is here! Spring is here!

—*Anon*

The Little Bird

A little bird, with feathers brown, sat singing on a tree;
The song was very soft and low, but sweet as it could be:
And all the people passing by looked up to see the bird
That made the sweetest melody that they had ever heard.

But all the bright eyes looked in vain, for birdie was so small,
And with a modest, dark brown coat, he made no show at all.
"Why Papa," little Effie said, "where can this birdie be?
If I could sing a song like that, I'd sit where folks could see."

"I hope my little girl will learn a lesson from that bird,
And try to do what good she can, not to be seen or heard.
This birdie is content to sit, unnoticed by the way,
And sweetly sing His Makers' praise from dawn to close of day.
So live, my child, all through your life, that, be it short or long,
Though others may forget your looks, they won't forget your song."

—Anon

White Crown

*And the eyes of them that see shall not be dim,
and the ears of them that hear shall hearken.*

—Isaiah 32:3

*I*t was while I was caught in a web of despair that I learned a new song—the scrumptious melody of the white-crowned sparrow. Had the bird not sung to me as I first opened my greenhouse, I would have missed the essence of the chronicle as my day unfolded. Neither Grace nor I had actually distinguished the song of this particular species before that very morning. To the untrained eye, this sparrow is just one among many plain brown birds. To the untrained ear, the song is difficult to distinguish from other species. In two different cities, two white-crown sparrows delivered a heavenly duet, to salve two aching hearts with a very specific message. It was no mere coincidence.

Not long ago I endured a complexity of difficulties that spiraled me downward, until I found myself in an unfamiliar emotional darkness. I look back on this experience as a time of desolation—a time when I was unable to discern even the hand of Providence. Even my greenhouse work among the fragrant, multi-colored flowers failed to lift my spirits. My eyes were closed to beauty, my ears did not want to hear my usual choice of sermon or soft music CDs. Silence was my solace. I found comfort in only one type of sound—bird songs!

Such Sweet Songs

Will I ever again experience the peace that used to come so naturally within my clear sacred walls? I wondered as I sped down the rocky country road on my quad instead of taking my usual vitalizing walk.

What kind of a day will this be? I wondered with a sigh as I lay back on my four-wheeler. I was physically tired, strained, empty. It was not a cloud-watching day. *Got to get the houses watered or I'll be behind all day.*

A tear might have escaped had it not been for the song. When it began, I opened my eyes and searched the branches above me, but I could not locate the singer. I lay there on my four-wheeler, wrapped in the thrill of the cheerful melody. I actually got goose bumps as I listened. My breathing slowed. My spirit was at rest.

Reluctantly, I roused from my reverie and slowly walked toward the Gardenhouse to check the tomatoes. When I opened the door I was greeted by a flutter of wings. A brown streak dove for refuge toward the fruit trees at the back of the greenhouse. Obviously, this little intruder had spent the night in my sanctuary. I often discover hummingbirds, chickadees, and juncos indoors. I once found a red-spot searching for insects among the semi-dwarf trees for awhile before I rolled up the sides to allow him to escape.

This was a cool morning, so I left the house enclosed while I watered the tomatoes. Within a minute or two, my bird of this morning began singing again, softly at first, and then with increasing enthusiasm, as if he were trying to out-sing the noise of the water pump. I stopped watering. In the ensuing quietness, the song, a series of smoothly orchestrated warbling, not unlike the splendid song of a canary, filled the chilly corners of the room and fed into my hungry soul. The co-mingled harmonies left me with the impression that there must be at least one other songster in the rafters. I looked up, but, no, it was just one, very plain-looking brown bird—sporting a few white streaks on his head. He sang for me until I finished watering the Gardenhouse and the sun came up. I rolled up the sides of the house and he flew away.

I'll always recognize the song of the white-crown sparrow. Everyone should have the joy of knowing that song. Why haven't I recognized it before?

White Crown

The watering done, breakfast eaten, the trailer packed with bedding plants and hanging baskets for town sales, and my morning spent transplanting seedlings, I stopped to rest on the patio in front of the main greenhouse before returning home for lunch. In the distance I heard the song of the white-crown. And then I heard a motor that signaled the arrival of Grace and her two children.

"I have been to several stores, and even a few greenhouses looking for sunflowers," Grace said dejectedly. "This morning you came to my mind."

"How many do you need?" I asked with a smile. This was the first year I had planted the fast-growers in several years, and they were in need of transplanting. I had, in fact, wondered that very morning why I had bothered to plant them.

"Oh! Do you have some, Linda?" When I showed her the gangly flowers she embraced the tray like a long-lost friend. "I truly did not think I would find any! But I didn't want to give up. These are just what I had in mind! I just have to have sunflowers this year!"

She chose a few more plants. I didn't have any change in the greenhouse, so I invited her to follow me uphill to the house. With business finished, I sensed her need to talk. I sent up a silent prayer to be able to listen and respond as needed. Grace settled back on the sofa and took a deep breath.

"The recent details of our lives are too involved to share," she began with a shake of her head. "But we are currently living in our camper, parked on our front lawn. I was so discouraged this morning, but as I was praying, I had a most interesting experience. A bird began singing just outside my open window. I slowly peeked through the curtains and discovered that the singer was a white-crown sparrow. The song filled my soul in a way that is difficult to describe. So much has been happening to our family that...well, I was really in need of that song!" When I told her about the white-crown sparrow singing in my Gardenhouse, she raised her eyebrows and smiled.

"Amazing! We listened to the same song this morning in two different towns!?"

Such Sweet Songs

"I am discovering that when people have ears to hear and eyes to see, birds can play an important role in healing," I explained, as much for my benefit as for hers. "I have three volumes of bird stories and am now collecting information for the fourth volume." I had a hunch that today's experience with Grace might possibly be part of the 'now' of which I spoke. "Do you like bird stories?" I asked.

"Love 'em."

I handed her Book One of my *On a Wing and a Prayer* series. She embraced it with enthusiasm.

"You wrote this?" She flipped open the book and read aloud from the page. It was the verse that accompanied a story entitled, "The Sparrow's Song."

> *"Are not five sparrows sold for two farthings,*
> *and not one of them is forgotten before God?*
> *But even the very hairs of your head are numbered.*
> *Fear not, therefore: ye are of more value than many sparrows."*

—Luke 12:6, 7

White Crown

"I can't believe it! This is exactly what I needed today!" Grace cried. Smiling and nodding, she thumbed the volume appreciatively.

"My husband suffered severe burns in this past month. I shared what I knew about Jed's burn experience with my family. Then, yesterday, when I discovered that the smoke alarm in our camper wasn't working, it seemed to reiterate that I should come and see you. Would you have some advice for me as my husband's care-giver?"

I reached for a copy of *Rainbow in the Flames*. When I handed it to her, she inhaled sharply. "Oh! Have you written Jed's story, too?" she queried. "Do I ever need this book! Maybe I will read it first!"

"I keep my copy of Jere's book, *You Can Survive!*, where it can remind me of the country home I am praying for. Your sunflowers will help me keep my country home in mind."

I reached for one more book. Grace read the title and sub title aloud. "*Country in My Heart:* success stories of people who prayed for a country home," and her "amazed" expression returned.

"How can you have every single book I need?"

"You will find these stories very encouraging, Grace. *Country in My Heart* is a compilation of stories written, for the most part, by folks who attended one of our Country Living seminars, decided they had to get out of the city, prayed earnestly, and soon found themselves in a country home."

With tears in her eyes, Grace arose and gave me a hug. So did the children. From the look in her eyes, I knew that she, too, sensed the awe of this divine appointment, like a rainbow of promise. Something good had happened. Something ordained; as if our angels had conferred together about the time and place of our rendezvous.

As I watched them round the bend, and out of sight, my own burdens were lighter. An array of words hovered in my mind, but they weren't quite all there, and the order eluded me. Eventually I would climb the stairway to uncover it.

Such Sweet Songs

*They may learn to hear His voice in the song of birds,
in the sighing of the trees, in the rolling thunder, and in the music of the sea.
And every object in nature will repeat to them His precious lessons.
To those who thus acquaint themselves with Christ,
the earth will nevermore be a lonely and desolate place.
It will be their Father's house, filled with the presence of Him who once
dwelt among men.*

—Ellen G. White

Re-reading the words, my heart was warmed. I thought, just maybe, I could feel the beginnings of a new song bubbling up to fill the dry and empty places in my heart.

―――――――――
*Not her real name

God, the Artist

God, when you thought of a pine tree,
How did you think of a star?
How did you dream of the Milky Way
To guide us from afar.
How did you think of a clean brown pool
Where flecks of shadows are?

God, when you thought of a cobweb,
How did you think of dew?
How did you know a spider's house
Had shingles bright and new?
How did you know the human folk
Would love them like they do?

God, when you patterned a bird song,
Flung on a silver string,
How did you know the ecstasy
That crystal call would bring?
How did you think of a bubbling throat
And a darling speckled wing?

God, when you chiseled a raindrop,
How did you think of a stem,
Bearing a lovely satin leaf
To hold the tiny gem?
How did you know a million drops
Would deck the morning's hem?

Why did you mate the moonlit night
With the honeysuckle vines?
How did you know Madeira bloom
Distilled ecstatic wines?
How did you weave the velvet disk
Where tangled perfumes are?
God, when you thought of a pine tree,
How did you think of a star?

—Angela Morgan

Bird Words

A group of birds is not always a flock! It can be…

A drift of quail

A dole of doves

A kit of pigeons

A cast of hawks

A siege of herons

A covey of grouse

A stand of plovers

A sord of mallards

A host of sparrows

A nye of pheasants

A murder of crows

A charm of finches

A tiding of magpies

A flight of swallows

A parliament of owls

A richesse of martens

An exaltation of larks

An unkindness of ravens

A murmuration of starlings

A gaggle of geese (in the air, a skein)

A lamentation of swans (in the air, a wedge)

Sweet Lesson of Trust

And the birds are teachers of the sweet lesson of trust.
Our heavenly Father provides for them;
but they must gather the food,
they must build their nests and rear their young.
Every moment they are exposed to enemies that seek to destroy them.
Yet how cheerily they go about their work!
How full of joy are their little songs!

—*Ellen G. White*

TEACH Services, Inc.
P U B L I S H I N G
www.TEACHServices.com • (800) 367-1844

We invite you to view the complete
selection of titles we publish at:
www.TEACHServices.com

We encourage you to write us
with your thoughts about this,
or any other book we publish at:
info@TEACHServices.com

TEACH Services' titles may be purchased in
bulk quantities for educational, fund-raising,
business, or promotional use.
bulksales@TEACHServices.com

Finally, if you are interested in seeing
your own book in print, please contact us at:
publishing@TEACHServices.com
We are happy to review your manuscript at no charge.

www.ingramcontent.com/pod-product-compliance
Lightning Source LLC
Chambersburg PA
CBHW020358170426
43200CB00005B/218